Sisters
of the Gift

Sisters
of the Gift

Lessons From the Classroom of Life

Gloria Sharpe Smith
Shelley M. Fisher, Ph.D.

Ernestine Meadows May
Doretha S. Rouse

XULON PRESS

Xulon Press
2301 Lucien Way #415
Maitland, FL 32751
407.339.4217
www.xulonpress.com

Sisters of the Gift
Lessons from the Classroom of Life

© 2022 by Gloria Sharpe Smith

You may access other books by the authors at Amazon.com
Or contact them at:
https://sistersofthegift.com

Paperback ISBN-13: 978-1-6628-4156-9
Hard Cover ISBN-13: 978-1-6628-4157-6
eBook ISBN-13: 978-1-6628-4158-3

Acknowledgement

With great honor and pleasure, we acknowledge Dr. Mildred C. Harris of God First Ministries, Chicago, Illinois, for being strategically placed in the body of Christ to help catapult us into this season of gifting to others from the impartations she has laid upon us in ministry, teaching, and fellowship in the sisterhood.

Dr. Harris, a woman of influence, has multi-faceted anointings, operating in the offices of the prophet, elder, teacher, minister, advisor, exhorter, and intercessor. She has worked unselfishly and tirelessly in ministry for over fifty years dedicating herself to the Will of the Father.

Dr. Mildred C. Harris is a retired kindergarten teacher and the author of several books.

The authors of this book esteem the gift of Christ in you!

Contents

Overcomers, By the Word

Prayers

Author Biographies

Introduction

In his book, *The Glory of Living* (2005), Dr. Myles Munroe states, "You and everyone on this planet are walking containers of His Glory, and it is the Creator's desire that each one releases that full Glory and fill the earth with the Glory of their Manufacturer." We have received the gift of God's grace of salvation through Jesus Christ, and we endeavor to proclaim it and offer that same gift to others through our stories in this book, *Sisters of the Gift*.

We are all connected, rarely are there any coincidences. We encounter various situations for a reason and in different seasons of life. We are individuals; each of us has been equipped with unique gifts and talents to share and put into action. This brings a sense of awareness that we are not designed to live out our lives in isolation but within a community. Each day, we are on stage, performing from a script that has been masterfully crafted to perpetuate goodness and responsibility. We are careful to show kindness, acceptance, and consideration because we are loved by God and called by God to love others. It is out of His love that this book, *Sisters of the Gift, Lessons from the Classroom of Life* has been written.

It is our hope that the stories in this book will inspire and encourage you to live and experience your own life from a different perspective and have new encounters with God. Here you will meet four women who were teachers in a Northwest Indiana public school system and were thrust together during a citywide custodial strike. As a direct result of this event, a Christian organization, Gary Educators for Christ, evolved. We bonded, grew, and became a connecting thread creating patterns that would have lasting impacts. Over a span of thirty years, we have had varied life experiences and have spent countless hours praying individually and together. We met weekly through our membership in the organization which provided us the opportunity to pray together for our students, families, various government and world leaders, and provide benevolent support to the community at large. We are all retired now and have hundreds of amazing stories and testimonies among us of how God never failed to meet us in the classroom of life with a lesson each day.

Life is full of twists and turns. Who could have imagined that friendships and spiritual growth would evolve from those meetings at the high school? But they did to the degree that wisdom and prayer gained prominence in our worldview. Commitment to God and to ourselves translated into wanting to serve and to pass on what we had learned. It did not matter that our backgrounds and spiritual experiences were as eclectic as a pattern in a fine tapestry. We found common ground in God.

Each of our stories bears witness of our faith in God; we present them here as our shared heritage forever. They have become the rejoicing of our hearts because our hope is in His Word that bears witness with every whisper, dream, and vision that we possess.

The Mantle of Judah hovers over Gloria Sharpe Smith, the visionary who has followed the voice of the Lord, to unite us for this project and to always go before Him with praise, bragging on His goodness and faithfulness with thanksgiving that He is God, our Father. "Surely the Lord does nothing but reveal his secret unto his servant the prophet" (Amos 3:7 NIV).

Dr. Shelley M. Fisher studies to "show herself approved as a workman rightly dividing the word of God," divinely proclaiming what is, and what is to come through prophecy.

Ernestine Meadows May, the dreamer, gives her ear to hear the call on her life to war in the heavenlies, calling upon the name of the Lord to fight in a spiritual battle to defeat the enemy declaring victory in Jesus. "Because greater is he that is in you than he that is in the world" (1 John 4:4 KJV).

"A three-fold cord is not quickly broken . . ." (Eccl. 4:12 KJV). The overlay to the cord is grace! Doretha Sturgis Rouse, affectionately known as "Sister Grace," brings the anointing of the Holy Spirit to the giving of thanks, making requests before God, and bearing the burden of the intercessor. Her passion is to help others by lifting a standard to the Lord in prayer.

To this end, our vision is to advance the Kingdom of God through reaching out to others, sharing words of inspiration and hope, and offering a moral and spiritual compass. Based on our experiences of overcoming by the words of our testimony, we hope that our readers can share in these experiences and know that God uses ordinary people to do extraordinary things!

Fathers,
Family,
Friendships

1

A Trophy Lesson

꧁

GLORIA SHARPE SMITH

Honor thy father and thy mother: that thy days may be long upon
the land which the Lord thy God giveth thee. (Ex. 20:12 KJV)

My spirit is dancing with joy as I recall a very special event that occurred sometime during my early childhood. Those memories are few; however, there are some standouts that flirt with my mind and contribute to shaping my view on the importance of "teachable moments." Such moments are essential in life and beneficial to both the student and the teacher; in this case, to the parent and the child.

Pictures can be a wonderful catalyst for stirring up memories and generating conversation. I have only one picture of myself as an infant and I cherish it. I don't know my exact age in the photo but the significance of it is that I'm in my mother's arms. It's just the two of us. She is young and beautiful, and I am a happy, full-faced, wide-eyed bundle of love. There's no picture of my dad and me because none exists. No one ever took one of the two of us. But, thanks to our heavenly Father, my mind captured and stored a picture of the only lesson that I recall my dad teaching me. He taught me how to give driving signals. I learned how to distinguish my left hand from my right. Thanks, Daddy! I got to experience my first and only "Take Your Daughter to Work Day" many years ago. My dad was a seasonal fruit picker when this lesson occurred in the late '40s. He picked oranges alongside many other black men who provided for their families through the Florida citrus industry. It was early morning on this particular day that my brother and I went to the orange grove with my dad. We were sitting on the front seat in the cab of the truck. I was beaming with excitement to be next to my dad while he was driving this long, flatbed, motor truck that was noted for transporting fine citrus fruit. As he was skillfully driving and slowly approaching a stop sign, he said, "Gloria Jean, I'm going to turn this corner, and this is how to signal if you're going to turn right or left." Then he went on to say, "If you're turning left, stick your arm out of the window and hold it straight out like this."

He demonstrated by holding up his left arm and then sticking it out of the window.

"Now, if you are going to turn right, stick your left arm out of the window and hold your hand up to the sky to signal that you're going to turn right."

He pointed out to me that my left arm was the only one that would ever go out of the window and the right arm would always be inside. I've neither forgotten that lesson, nor its importance. Oftentimes, when I'm driving or giving directions to others, I remember it and whisper, "Thank you, Daddy."

He taught me a valuable lesson, one that he knew I would need for a lifetime. That day, he made his young daughter feel very special and loved. I believe God, our heavenly Father, orchestrated this lesson because He knew then that I would need a warm, loving memory of my childhood relationship with my dad. The picture of this significant lesson (left from right) is forever imprinted as a memory in my mind.

God's Homework: Recall a memory from your own childhood for which there is no picture to document. Write about it. Describe your feelings.

2

Listen to Your Daddy When You Don't Have One!

ERNESTINE MEADOWS MAY

If you then, being evil, know how to give good gifts to your children, how much more will your Father who is in heaven give good things to those who ask Him. (Matt. 7:11 KJV)

Down in the meadow in an itty-bitty pool, swam two little fishies and the mother fish too. "Swim!" said the mama fish. "Swim, if you can" And they swam and they swam all over the dam! "Stop," said the mother fish, "or you will get lost" The three little fishies didn't want to be bossed. The three little fishies went off on a spree and they swam, and they swam right out to the sea— lyrics by Josephine Carringer and Bernice Idens (1939)

In this catchy little rhyming song meant for early elementary school aged children, we can see the clear lesson to listen, be obedient, and be wise! Notice how the song makes no mention of a daddy fish. We can surmise that daddy wasn't around anymore—or perhaps he just didn't come along for the swim. Whatever the case, mama fish, as in many households today, is the lead parent when it comes to raising the children in the family. And honestly, if everything was left up to us to order in our own way in life, we would most likely swim over the dam as well. However, even though we are given a free choice and range to express how our lives will be lived according to many options, there is more at play.

Born into this world without the blessings of my natural father, as he had preceded me in death, I had an unspoken confidence about myself growing up. Although there was already a breach in my family unit, I became acquainted with father figures on the front line, where I determined to be sent by God. I had a caring and wonderful stepfather, our church minister, and the president of the junior college I attended. It took me many years to come to the realization of the value of fatherhood and what it means to have this particular figurehead available as a stronghold as it is needed.

As a child, one of the first lines of Scripture I learned came from the twenty-third Psalm. "The Lord is my shepherd, I shall not want" (Ps. 23:1). It was imperative, at that time, that every believer affirm their faith in God by declaring the Word from the Ancient of times. Whether it was at the dinner table, in Sunday School, or even at school, it was a requirement. As a five- or six-year-old-child, I really didn't know the deeper side of the Bible, but I was beginning, in a small way, to speak the Word aloud into my own ears and as a result my faith would grow. Declaring the Word was important to all who required this of me. Later in life, I would not depart from what I had hidden in my heart.

This I now know: that a shepherd has a relationship with his flock and, if necessary, he would lay down his life for them. He also knows each sheep by name, as well as recognizing every blemish and mark on their bodies.

I grew up in a culture where the norms established by family law were accepted without questions. I listened to everything that was taught at home or church. I had my own reservations about some things, but I kept them to myself. I often heard my older sisters and brothers talk about our daddy, as they remembered him. I held what they said within my heart. I tried to visualize how he would call me his baby girl and how he would have loved and protected me. Afterall, that's what fathers do. I learned that he took care of his family, in part, by unconventional means. We were seven siblings. One job was insufficient to care for a family of nine. He was an independent village blacksmith, a small farmer, and a poker enthusiast who played for the interest he had in the game. I was told that he was good at the game. Apparently, he had a way of bringing home the bounties befitting a winner!

It was expected that I would follow the teachings of the Bible and the standards of behavior set by mama in our home. We, as children, had the awesome responsibility to help our parents earn a living by working in the fields, from the smallest to the greatest among us! I secretly prayed that, if there was a God in heaven, that He would get me out of this situation! I knew I would be there until I finished high school unless a miracle happened. It looked as though I would be stuck at home for a while. I didn't know that, behind my back, my heavenly Father had a different plan for me. He would work behind the scenes to perfect all things, in the absence of my earthly father, for my expected end!

During the last summer following high school graduation, my principal asked about my plans for college. I had no means to entertain this possibility. However, I was anticipating that something would happen. I just didn't know what it could be. In my head, it was not college. My principal offered me an idea to ponder. He had an old college buddy who had just been appointed president of a junior college in North Little Rock, Arkansas. He proposed to me that he give his buddy a call to see if I could be enrolled on a work-aid scholarship. I did not allow my hopes to overcome me with anxiety.

The proposed plan became a reality. As for finances, I had none. My momma could not afford to send me to any college, because she had no money either. Share crop farming allowed families to break even at the end of the harvesting season. Normally, we raised our own vegetables. My daddy had planted a fruit orchard early in my parents' marriage that yielded many different fruits, he left us with several heads of castle that were of great value also. Basic pantry items and staples were put on credit until the end of the season. Nevertheless, we always had more than enough provisions, because of my momma's dependency on God.

Things began to fall in place for me as I went out into the world. But as you already know, I was not on my own! Not only did I enroll in the junior college on a work-aid scholarship, but the president of the college put me in a position to be his personal secretary. I was just out of high school, with two years of typing class, but I felt if he wanted to hire me, I was willing to take it on. As it turned out, he helped me to become acclimated into that role. He was a wonderful, Godly man.

At the completion of my two years at the junior college level, I transferred to a four-year college. I enrolled again without any money. Arrangements were made for me to apply for a student loan. It was what I needed to complete my education. The loan carried a rider that stated that there was a caveat for repayment. If I were to be employed by a school system that was recognized as a low income, or Title One, my loan could be reduced by 50 percent! I decided that was the course I would pursue. Years later, as my payments for the loan came due, I made the first two installments as demanded, and months later I received a communication from the college that the balance of my loan had been canceled. My first teaching assignment, after moving to Indiana, qualified me and had given validation to the rider.

I did not recognize the level of favor that was being directed on my behalf by my heavenly Father. I just thought life was that good to me! But it was the Lord, Himself, who connected me to these father figures: my wonderful step-father, my surrogate grandfather, my principal, my college president, and my spiritual father (who played a pivotal role in my life as a father).

The gaps and voids are closed in our lives when we acknowledge God as our provision. He leaves no footprints when He's on our turf, but He leaves a lasting imprint on our hearts. It's the imprint that relates to victorious living. That's who our Father is!

My thoughts direct me to Philippians 4:8, which tells us to think of things that are just pure, lovely, commendable, beautiful, excellent, or praise-worthy, which requires a disciplined life.

I would sometimes become disappointed, just because life happens. It is the plan of the enemy to distract us and take our focus away from our Father's will. In life, there are no shortages of hurts and disappointments promised to us. But when we feel impacted by these emotions, there are adjustments, compromises, understanding, and a line of open and positive communication available to us that are necessary to toggle through. We must always remember that we can trust the faithful, the unshakeable, the One who is always constant. I remember thinking often about how I never had a daddy to run to for comfort, protection, and advice. While I was trying to it all out, all wrapped up in myself, I heard His voice inwardly delivering a loving rebuke, "*Stop crying. I am your heavenly Father!*"

Those words have resonated with me until this day, because He removed my burdens and made His yoke easy for me. It was profound. The end result has been sustained peace, caring, and a divine relationship. I understand more and more each day that every good and perfect gift to me is from my Father above.

He has a plan for our lives and provides seamless transitions from worry to joy if we can only believe. To this end He has already mitigated every situation and circumstance that easily threatens our faith when He gave His life for us at the cross. He declared, "It is finished!" He is faithful to His Word and His unconditional love lifts us up and gives us hope. Even in these my later days, He is still fulfilling His promises. Why should we be sad? Why should we shed tears when His comfort and His peace live within us?

I know now to depend on my heavenly Father for all my needs in life according to His sustainability! His plan for me is a good one: to prosper me in good health, even as my soul prospers; He gives me an expected end, and I have learned to trust Him as I enter each day in anticipation of His loving kindness and His good will for me! In Him, I will not yield to disappointment. I will defer to His promised word to comfort me. When my emotions rise up to overcome me, He makes me lie down in green pastures because it is His good pleasure to comfort me, to nourish me, and to provide for my every need and desire! Thank you, Abba. You are my shepherd and I shall have no want of anything! "You supply all of our needs according to your riches and glory by Christ Jesus." He desires for you to come to Him in the same way. He wants to cover you with His feathers. He wants to protect you and comfort you with His everlasting love! Say His name! He is our Ultimate Father and we should listen to our Daddy, because He loved us to the death of His Son.

I declare and decree that in your search for the how's, why's, when's, or where's in your life that Father God will begin to speak to your heart, convincing you that surely goodness and mercy shall follow you all the days of your life, being, "predestined according to the purpose of Him who works all things after the counsel of His own will" (Eph. 11 KJV). Amen.

God's Homework: Recall a fun time you had as a child and sing a catchy song that perhaps children do not sing today.

3

The Man in the Sailor Suit

～✦～

SHELLEY M. FISHER, PH.D.

*For the word of God is quick, and powerful, and sharper than
any two-edged sword, piercing even to the dividing of soul
and spirit, and of the joints and marrow, and is a discerner of
the thoughts and intents of the heart.* (Heb. 4:12 NKJV)

*The Navy Man had a wife, a boy, and a girl.
The war was over so—was
the life of the family of four.
There was a divorce.
The family of four was no more.*
—Shelley M. Fisher

M y parents divorced when I was three, but I did not know it. I
can only remember events from the age of five, when Mom
married again. I was always excited to visit my grandmother's
home. It was there I saw the picture of the man in the sailor suit.
Grandmother told stories of when he was a young boy. I can even
remember writing letters to the sailor, but I never mailed them.

The sailor was my dad. I longed to have a relationship with him,
although I had a good relationship with my stepfather. There was
just something in me that longed to connect the human with the
photo. In retrospect, I realize I never voiced my feelings to anyone.
I wore a façade that transmitted the message, "All is well." As I

grew up, the man in the sailor suit made promises to come and get my brother and me to take us on outings with him. Sometimes he would keep the engagements, but most times he would not. When he visited, he always had some strange lady with him, and he often seemed more interested in the lady than my brother and me.

After graduating from college, I went to see the man in the sailor suit. By then, he lived in a neighboring state. He and his wife took me fishing. All night long they sat on the riverbank, while I slept on a nearby bench. I just could not identify with fishing at such a weird hour when people were supposed to be sleeping. They fished until the wee hours of the morning and . . . no fish.

I was married with two children and decided to take a creative writing course at the local university. I was thirty-fours years old. There were seven of us in the class. We were meant to write on specific topics and discuss our work together. I wrote an awful story about a girl named Meredith who went fishing with her dad and slept the night away.

I can remember the comments made by the other writers more than I recall the content of the story. A blonde, blue-eyed nineteen-year-old girl looked directly at me and said, "I think you're Meredith. I think you're thumbing your nose at your dad, saying, 'I made it without you. Look at me now.'" My heart started pounding and felt as though it might leap from my chest. I realized she was right on. Up to and until then, I had never realized how much I resented my dad.

It is funny how this "biological dad" thing seemed settled but would resurface out of nowhere. A memorable event took place at a grief counseling session at church. I had attended the session, excited to glean techniques from my pastor and a clinical psychologist. I, personally, wanted to institute the practice of helping people overcome or manage grief. My position was that of associate minister, consequently, I preached, led prayer, and taught workshops for our congregants and, also, other churches.

During one session, there were about twenty-five people seated in a semicircle. My husband and I sat near the front, close to the pastor and clinical psychologist. A lady I did not recognize came in and took the seat to my right. She was not a member of the church. She introduced herself to the group and quietly announced that her father had recently died. Someone had told her about the session, and she had decided to participate.

The pastor and psychologist began explaining that grief included more than a death. It could also be caused by the separation of various entities who were familiar to a person. Warm tears began to fall down my cheeks. I heard the lady to my right whimpering. Before long, I was crying aloud. The more I tried to shut things down, the louder I became. The lady to my right hit higher decibels with her crying. The two of us were simultaneously boo-hooing profusely. The room became quiet, probably because no one could be heard over our crying.

I lost it, me—the church leader who taught, preached, and prayed for congregants . . . the wife and mother . . . the educator-by-profession. I was one of two protagonists blubbering in the semicircle. I guess I could have been embarrassed, but I was not. In a way, I was glad to have had the lady to my right sobbing uncontrollably in concert with me. The experience released a peace within my core being that I had never experienced. I felt lightweight, as though I were floating on a cloud.

Grief can be held unknowingly. I had hidden mine in the crevices of my being and suddenly released it from captivity. My subconscious mind had overpowered my conscious behavior into thinking that all was well when in actuality all was hidden, denied by me. God is a discerner of the thoughts and intents of the heart (Heb. 4:12 NKJV). He knows us better than we know ourselves. This was my time to be set free from the grief that I had stashed away in my heart.

A significant milestone with the man in the sailor suit occurred when I received a phone call from an unknown woman living in a nearby city who told me my father's wife had died. She simply stated that he needed me. By this time, my heart was softened. I went to his rescue, helping him dispose of his belongings and moving him into an assisted-living arrangement. I hired a geriatric social worker to oversee his care. He was in the beginning stages of Alzheimer's disease. I talked my brother, who at first did not want to see our father, into visiting our dad.

Helping our dad manage the transition from the assisted living to the nursing home, my brother and I reconciled with our dad. I was able to understand what had happened to him and minister to him. He had not been "fathered," so he did not know how to be a father to my brother and me. Looking back, I realize our journey was no accident. I believe God orchestrated our reconciliations before our father's death. It was His gift to me. I was allowed resolution and could look at the photo of the man in the sailor suit with satisfaction.

God's Homework: You have a Father who ordained your relationships and success before the foundation of the earth. Receive the love of your heavenly Father to get you through any and all circumstances. He loves you and is waiting for you to fall into His arms and receive Him.

4

Fully Validated

❧

GLORIA SHARPE SMITH

For I know the plans I have for you, declares the LORD, "plans
to prosper you and not to harm you, plans to give you hope and a
future. Then you will call upon me and come and pray to me, and I
will listen to you. You will seek me and find me when you seek me
with all your heart. I will be found by you," declares the LORD,
and will bring you back from captivity. (Jer. 29:11–14 NIV)

G rowing up, I didn't know God as my heavenly Father. My dad
didn't provide the affirmation that I needed to mature, be
courageous, have confidence, and feel love and acceptance. Neither
he nor I knew the impact that this upbringing would have on me.
But it was all a part of a uniquely designed master plan for my life.

Frankfurt, Kentucky. Freedom! College life; first time away
from home; dormitory living; campus activities, movies, make up,
nail polish, lipstick, a steady boyfriend, an engagement ring, and a
husband; all in the span of two years after leaving the place that I
had called home for the first sixteen years of my life.

My grandmother, Olivia, was the catalyst for me attending
the college. She had attended Morris Brown College in Atlanta
for a year when she was younger, but she dropped out because of
hunger. Her father was a railroad worker and she had always had
food to eat at home. That wasn't the case for her at Morris Brown.
Her story line mostly went like this: "Gloria Jean, I just never got

enough to eat there." She let me know this truth with a serious shake of her head.

Grandmother Olivia missed her parents and food. She begged her dad to allow her to return home. With both parents consenting, she left Morris Brown and never returned to complete her college education. Instead, she let that desire for a college education, and the fruit of its reward, become a dream and a goal for me to achieve. I was never hungry at Kentucky State and always had sufficient money. She made sure that I had everything that she thought I needed.

"Stay in school." Those were the words of encouragement that she often spoke to me along with: "Gloria Jean, just trust in the Lord."

I stayed in college until 1964, long enough to meet and marry Ernest T. Smith, my college sweetheart. We shared a love for life and each other for fifty-two years. He passed away on March 1, 2017. He was the ideal husband who I believe God had chosen for me and he was a wonderful dad to our two sons.

My personal encounter with my heavenly Father occurred as I was walking down Ellis Avenue in Chicago, Illinois. I was on my way to work.

Out of nowhere, I heard my name, *"Gloria."*

I knew it was the voice of God.

Immediately, I said, "God, where are you?"

And instantly, reflecting on the Sunday sermon that focused on walking with God and keeping Him close, I asked the question, "Why did you leave me?"

He answered, "I never left you. You left me. I've been with you all the time."

I didn't even realize that He cared that I had stopped my hypocritical worship from my youth, teen, and young adult years. Sure, I had read stories about God and Jesus. I had even heard about the Holy Spirit because I had been a regular church girl. I had even taught Sunday school for a while. So, I believed that He existed, but I never had a personal encounter with Him until then.

After this encounter, my life changed. I began to read the Bible that Grandmother Olivia had sent to me years earlier. It had always been on display on the coffee table, but it was never read. I started to get to know Him. I invited Jesus Christ into my heart and asked Him to lead me and teach me how to live and love life the way He wanted me to. Of course, I asked to be forgiven of my sins and wrongdoings, so to speak, and that happened. I received the forgiveness that His love and grace offered. A new life was now mine. God has blessed me with peace and trust and also with a hope that goes beyond anything I could have imagined as a young girl.

I always remember that it was my earthly father who gave me my name, *Gloria Jean,* which means "Glory to God." The Lord is gracious. I get to live freely each day in the presence of my heavenly Father and experience His amazing grace and His love for me. And it's all because of the personal relationship that I enjoy with Him today.

God's Homework: Make a side-by-side list of the traits of both your earthly father and your heavenly Father. What characteristics are you grateful for?

5

A Call to Fatherhood

~✦~

ERNESTINE MEADOWS MAY

Love covers a multitude of sins. (1 Peter 4:8 KJV)

*This story is dedicated to the memory of a little girl who touched
our hearts during her short life here on God's earth. She brought
with her a wealth of potential and hope for a future with great
expectations! I know He sent her to show the world about
unconditional and unclaimed love. Heaven is now her home!*

Dee was about five years old when I found out that she and
my son shared the same dad. That was my ex-husband. This
was a call for transparency! I reveal this story in the hopes that
it will help anyone who has developed a cold relationship with a
husband or a significant other because of a child who has come
into the family equation without the benefit of a welcome mat.
Hurt, disappointment, anger, brokenness, and a myriad of other
emotions could possibly be the culprit that precipitates arguments,
fights, or a prolonged distancing within these relationships.

Whatever past conditions had been set, I recognized that
I was meant to help break the pattern of separation between
daughter and father. Seeking answers to questions was not my
quest. And of course, shame and guilt are sometimes the com-
ponents of such a separation. Without any intention to be judg-
mental or pushy to make this union happen, I understood that

there was more at stake. There was a possibility for a wonderful relationship to be born. I felt that the goodness of His Spirit was moving me forward. I appointed myself as God's mediator. I wanted Dee to know her brother, and even better . . . her biological father. I wanted her to know that she was loved and that she had a place in her father's life. The more I thought of her, the more I wanted to meet her. I felt the prodding of the Holy Spirit's love being released into these unions. The Bible says, in James 1, "Let patience have her perfect work..." (James 1:3–4 KJV). I prayed it would be so.

Time was passing and I could not even imagine the thoughts that were going through her dad's mind. Maybe they were along the lines of acceptance or resentment. All I knew was there was a little sweetheart without the benefit of her father's bond and love. I wanted to do the right thing, creating a gentle and caring environment for us all.

> *The nature of impending fatherhood is that you are doing something that you're unqualified to do, and then you become qualified while doing it.*
> —John Green, American author

The time had finally come that Dee would make our home hers. At age six, she was as pretty as her picture and smart and proper in her speech. She seemed happy to get to know us and the feelings were mutual. She and my son, Andre, got along very well. He was two. She was not treated as a stranger in our household. She was introduced to the other members of the family. She went about as though she had been there since birth. God is so awesome in all His ways. He knows the ending from the beginning! "He gives us the desires of our hearts" (Ps. 37:4). In essence, He plants those desires and then we come into the realization that the blessings began with Him! Dee was in love with her Aunt Helen and wanted to walk half the block down to her house every visit she made. She was never a transplant. She was destined to be a part of our family.

Life is short! I say to you this day, keep loved ones dear to your heart. Let them know you are there for them. Bless them with your prayers. I must reiterate—life is short!

Dee finished high school and went on to college. I was informed that, upon graduating, she had taken a job working at one of the televisions stations in Little Rock, Arkansas. She went home after work one evening, laid across her bed never to awaken again. What a heartbreak for everyone! So unexpected! I didn't know how to handle the grief. I'd had no further contact with Dee after her father and I had divorced. I had to get past all of the unanswered questions, but even today I think of such a sweet and endearing child, so full of potential to orchestrate a wholesome and rewarding life. Her sudden, unexpected death still confounds me. Only God knows why. I accepted this and reached for His peace. God fulfilled a desire to know and love her for her short time on earth. Looking back, I celebrate that He is a God of peace and restoration.

I thank Him for the time we shared with Dee. I feel privileged to have seen how love and forgiveness were wrapped up in a little child. She was a beautiful example sent to show and teach us the ways of God, our Father. Children come clothed in innocence, without blame, that we should cast no blame or shame upon them.

Again, I say, life is short. There is only one perfect Father and that is our Father in heaven. Perfection is never attained here on earth, but it is a process that will be realized in the day of Jesus Christ, our Lord and Savior. It is imperative that we make the decision to let go of stuff and live life in a loving and accepting way, just as a little child. If necessary, be the conduit for a father and daughter or son to be reconciled. Love is active! Accept the unconditional love of our Father in order to respond to this world by loving others accordingly.

Remember these promises and instructions when it becomes hard to bear the vicissitudes that come in your life" "His yoke is easy and His burden is light" (Matt. 11:30); "Cast all of your cares on Him for He cares for you" (1 Peter 5:7); "Fathers, . . . bring them up in the nurture and admonition of the Lord" (Eph. 6:4).

Unforgiveness is a burden to carry. It is a yoke that hangs heavily on your neck, just as the burden carried by work oxen. If we struggle, we can meditate on His guidance, "Forgive that your Father in Heaven may forgive you" (Matt. 6:14).

God's Homework: In addition to your biological father, think of a male figure in your life who you have looked up to and who encouraged you in some special way. Send a "thank you" through text, email, or social media. Or . . . why not take the extra step of writing a personalized note?

6

My Introduction to Isaiah

༺✶༻

SHELLEY M. FISHER, PH.D.

The time is fulfilled, and the kingdom of God is at hand.
Repent and believe in the gospel. (Mark 1:15 NKJV)

I was curious about God. I felt that there was more to Him than what I was seeing in my denominational church. The teacher/ leader of our group, Gary Educators for Christ, emphasized prayer and developing an intimate relationship with Him. I believed the timing was right for me; that this was my *kairos* moment to know God in a deeper sense. After all, the Bible says the sons of Issachar knew the times and seasons (2 Chron. 12:32 author's paraphrase).

Several months prior to that meeting at the high school, I had opened my Bible and begun pondering the Scripture, Mark 1:15. I was attending church and I believed I was a good person. What could God be saying to me in this Scripture: "The time is fulfilled, and the kingdom of God is at hand; repent ye and believe the gospel." I believed in God and had already been baptized. Though I did not think I was a bad person, the words "repent and believe the gospel" continually leapt at me. I would just reach for my Bible, open it, and there on the page was Mark 1:15.

I studied Romans 10, the Scripture that leads to your receiving salvation, for three consecutive months. It states, "That if you con- fess with your mouth the Lord Jesus and believe in your heart that God has raised Him from the dead, you will be saved. For with the heart one believes unto righteousness, and with the mouth confession is made unto salvation" (Rom. 10:9–10). I was diligent to confess this and asked for the forgiveness of all my sins. I believed the Lord guided me to these verses so that this task would be completed and enhance my spiritual life.

It was then that I saw I had the greatest Father possible all along, my heavenly Father. With this understanding, I began to read Scriptures that told me who I was (and still am) and what I have in Christ Jesus. For example, I Corinthians 5 tells me of my inheritance in Christ starting with a new beginning: "Wherefore if any man is in Christ Jesus, he is a new creature and all things have become new" (I Cor. 5:17). My old deeds and sins have been blotted out and I embark upon this "newness," a new start in Christ Jesus.

The Word of God began to have new meaning for me. My leader and mentor kept teaching us about prayer and the importance of studying God's Word. Our mentor was also preaching and prophesying.

After one particular meeting, she came over to me and a friend, saying to me, "You will preach the Word all over your city. People will know who you are. Your name will be in newspapers."

I heard her and I thought, *"Who?"*

I turned and looked behind me, thinking she was talking to someone else. But she got my attention again by calling my name.

She said, "I'm talking to you."

I sounded like an owl, as I continued to question, "Who! Who?"

She said, "Yes, you."

From that moment on, a new resolve, a greater thirst, enveloped me concerning the Word. I began to study more, get quiet more, and this was when I met Isaiah. I was not ready to tell my husband about Isaiah yet, during our initial meeting, because I did not think he would understand. I am eager, though, to share the story with you.

I do not recall how I arrived at Isaiah 6 in my Bible, but I very quickly became stuck there, so much so that I learned to quote it in its entirety. It was in my system. I was particularly compelled to quote the words, "In the year that King Uzziah died, I saw the glory of the Lord high and lifted up…" (Isa. 6:1 KJV).

Before long, I was invited to churches to speak at their morning services. I was sought after to speak to women's groups. I spoke at the morning service at my own church. I can remember forming a mental strategy early on, thinking to myself, *I do not know what I am doing, but I am going to behave as though I do.*

Apparently, my plan worked. After service at my local church, a parishioner came up to me and said, "You sound like you really know what you're talking about."

I want you to recognize that God is no respecter of persons. He uses ordinary people to do extraordinary things, supernatural things. I believe that we meander through life until God nudges us into a new path to do his bidding on the earth. From this start, intercessory prayer became my priority. Through that, God used Isaiah 6 to call me into ministry. He waited patiently until I finished my here-and-there-and-everywhere activities. He reached me through my mentor and the prophet Isaiah. God thrusts people across your path to get you to move where He wants you to be, so that you can listen, hear, and obey Him. He has a destiny waiting for you to fulfill.

Isaiah 1:9 says if we are willing and obedient, we will eat the good of the land. Trust God and rely on Him. He does the calling and makes the assignments. He Who begins a good work in you is able to finish it. When God calls you, He will provide. It is all about Him and how He wants to use you. Yield to Him and He will open treasures to you.

Give God your attention. Is there a particular Scripture or words from the Bible that seem to demand your attention? It is no accident. God is speaking to you. In your quiet time, purpose to hear His Voice, then obey. He will take you places you never dreamed of, or have you doing things that you thought impossible. Yield to His voice.

God's Homework: Before reading your Bible, pray and ask God to speak to you. He has a destiny pre planned for you. By entering in relationship with Him—reading, meditating the Word, getting in His presence, you will know your assignment. Listen, then obey.

7

Ultimate Trust

❧

GLORIA SHARPE SMITH

Trust in the Lord with all thine heart; and lean not
unto thine own understanding. (Prov. 3:5 KJV)

These words are skillfully written on a round, fluted-edge plate that is displayed on a small, wooden easel in my living room: "A friend is God's way of proving He doesn't want us to walk alone." The author is cited as "unknown" and the dish was a gift from my dear friend, Dot. We met while attending a birthday party for my godson's daughter. She and her husband had recently moved to Texas, and so had we. Friendship was just what the four of us needed. We loved the state but didn't have any friends our age in the area.

As life progresses, Dot and I have continued to build a wonderful relationship. In fact, it is just the kind that I always seem to need at various stages of my life. She's a very spiritual, kind, and thoughtful woman. We share common beliefs in the basic principles of life. Our values are aligned with the Bible. In other words, she is a gift to me.

The words on the plate that Dot (she prefers the nickname) gave me remind me that friendships are a necessary part of life and also that each one has a significant role. When I look back at the various friendships that I've entertained from my early childhood, throughout my youth and teenage years, and even as a young married woman, each has been different, yet rewarding. There is value within each friendship and they have all enabled me to have many unforgettable experiences. I would like to tell you about one in particular. I fondly remember it as my first, and only, water skiing lesson.

My late husband, Ernest, and I eloped on June 27, 1964. He was from Louisville, Kentucky, and I from Orlando, Florida. After he graduated college, he landed a job in Indianapolis as an Industrial Arts teacher in a middle school. At the time, I was still a college student. During Christmas break, we had a formal church wedding ceremony on December 26, 1964, in Orlando. Following this, we traveled to Indianapolis and moved into our first apartment.

My husband met a fraternity brother who also worked at the same middle school. They were immediate friends. On a day that I will always remember, Mason invited Ernest to have lunch at his home and to bring me along to meet his wife, Beverly. She was also the complex apartment manager. When Ernest and I arrived at their apartment for lunch, she was not at home as she was investigating a tenant's concern across the campus complex. Interestingly, her absence consequently caused our first meeting to occur inside an awkward situation. Mason instructed Ernest and me to make ourselves comfortable. Additionally, he asked me to take a look at the chicken that was baking in the oven. I proceeded to do as he requested. That's when Bev walked in to find me in her kitchen with the oven door open and, I'm certain, a startled look on my face.

She immediately began laughing and said, "Well, who is this?"

Mason introduced me to her as Ernest's wife. I asked her why she was laughing. Turns out, she found the whole thing to be comical because Mason didn't know how to cook and had to have a person he barely knew, me, checking the chicken. Our introduction brought us many laughs and was the beginning of an amazing friendship for the four of us as well as the six children between us, friendships that have never wavered.

Now, I can imagine you might be wondering, *What does any of this have to do with water skiing?* Beverly was a nurse by profession and also a certified lifeguard. We all enjoyed family camping and looked forward to every weekend, when we would travel to some nearby campground and enjoy life in its finest environment—the splendid outdoors. Our family unit consisted of four adults and three children at the time of my skiing lesson.

On this particular August weekend, we'd loaded up the car with all of the gear and hitched the pop-up camper to the back of our Pontiac LeMans. How we all managed to share space inside that small trailer is still an accomplishment that warms my heart. We also towed a boat for our pleasure. Our destination of choice was Lake Geneva, Wisconsin. We traveled safely to the campground that Friday and on Saturday morning after a light breakfast, we were ready to take the boat out. Everything was perfect and the kids were in the care of a teen-aged babysitter. We brought her along to afford us the opportunity to enjoy the night life in the popular tourist town.

While launching the boat, we discovered that the water was ice cold, but that fact did nothing to deter us from having a relaxing cruise on the lake. Nothing could top the giant mosquitos that we had encountered the night before while setting up the trailer and tent at the campground.

I was enjoying every aspect of my first boat ride on Lake Geneva when Mason shouted out, "How about trying out those skis, Gloria?"

"Who me?" was my initial reply. Laughing at the ludicrous suggestion, I added, "I've never been on water skis before, and besides, I don't know how to swim!"

Before the sound of my voice and laughter subsided, Beverly yelled out, "You don't have to know how to swim. You can do it!"

I was filled with excitement, but my mind was in conflict. *Is she crazy? I can't swim. I'm wearing contact lenses. Look at ALL of that water!* But my heart was dancing with every beat and saying, *"Go for it!"* I remembered the words that my grandmother Olivia would often use to encourage me. "Trust in the Lord!" she'd always say.

With those words, and Beverly's presence and confidence in me, I donned the bright orange life vest and said to Bev, "I'm putting my life in your hands!"

She responded, "I'm not going to let you *drown!*"

She honored my trust and confidence by getting into the water first and beckoning me to follow. We both held onto the long ski rope, as she assisted me in putting on the slim, cumbersome skis. I was ready to experience a thrill that I knew instinctively I would never forget. My husband was seated in the boat with Mason in calm disbelief, I'm sure, that this was really happening.

All the while, Mason was cheering me on by repeating, "Let's get this girl up on those skis!"

I was ready.

Beverly began to give me instructions.

"Okay, while holding onto the rope, squat like you're trying to sit. Keep your arms straight out in front of you. I'm going to hold the tip of the skis. You can see they are up, out of the water. While you're squatting, keep your legs together just close enough to stand up later with a slight bend in your knees."

She further reiterated that when I was in perfect position, she would tell Mason to drag us slowly through the water, so that she could go with me until I got up. I felt she was all of the security I needed.

With me in position and Beverly close by, she yelled, "Hit it!"

I realized almost immediately that she meant for Mason to start the motor. The boat was about fifty feet away from us. I could see that the long rope, which I was holding on to for dear life, was securely attached to the boat. I could hear the roaring of the motor. I could see the waves being aroused in the water as I was being pulled through it. I began to follow Bev's instructions and almost, without much effort, I was up and water skiing for the first time in my life. It was a successful, exhilarating experience. I had trusted Bev completely. She had exhibited total confidence in me. We celebrated my victory together. I came up on the skis on the first try and stayed up for about half a mile on the water. The Lord was with me and I felt amazing!

Before I could fully digest what had just happened, Mason was there with the boat to rescue me and said, "Let's do it again, that was great!"

The second time up, I skied even farther. I made it look so easy that my husband decided that he would give it a try. His lesson didn't go the same as mine. He was never able to get up on the skis as I had done.

My friendship with Beverly is a blessing from God. We've both enjoyed it immensely. The Lord smiled on us during that water skiing lesson and cemented a bond between us that cannot be destroyed. When you place trust, confidence, and encouragement in someone, wonderful results can happen, and lasting relationships can be made.

Beverly spoke a very odd truth to me when she said, "You don't need to know how to swim to ski."

She was right. I didn't doubt her confidence in me, nor did she doubt my ability. She offered me encouragement, and, by God's grace, I didn't disappoint her.

During the years, we've shared many other memorable times and experiences. They have included being pregnant at the same time, raising our children together as cousins, attending weddings, funerals, parties, graduations, vacations, and all of the other experiences that come with living a full blessed life. Although we did not always live in Indianapolis at the same time, we've maintained our friendship and managed camping trips and Thanksgiving every year.

Some of life's most precious gifts come to us in friendships. I'm so grateful for each one that I've been blessed to have. God really does not want us to walk alone. He chooses people to walk beside us. I know His choices are intentional and purposeful. I know He has enabled Bev and me to remain friends for both His glory and our delightful enjoyment. It has never mattered to either of us that I'm black and Beverly is white. God loves both of us and our hearts have been knitted together by Him. Do you have a friendship that you cherish and can see it as the gift it's meant to be?

God's Homework: Contact a dear friend today and reminisce about a special moment you've shared.

8

Who's Your Friend?

ERNESTINE MEADOWS MAY

And as you wish that others would do to
you, do so to them. (Luke 6:3 ESV)

W hen you think of a friend, you think of someone with
whom you share a bond or mutual affection, a natural
affinity or attraction. My disclaimer, for the sake of this story, will
let you know that we can also find friends outside the range of age,
interest, or shared bond. I don't doubt that we all need someone
with whom we can share our secrets, find compassion, secure a
stamp of approval, and receive acceptance.

For some reason, I did not make a strong connection with a
lot of kids during my childhood. Perhaps it was because, many
times, we were not in close proximity to other families. It might
have been that I didn't need an attachment to become what I was
destined in life to be. Attachments, in the form of friends, can
hold you back if they are not corresponding dreamers, believers,
thinkers, and doers as you are. We moved around a lot. And I *was*
happy when we had the blessing of being near families with children who came with that move.

It was, and I think still is, an assumption that your level of popularity in high school declared how many friends you had. I cared
nothing about the system. I gave myself approval that my comfort
zone would reside with my *"ace vou coui"* (our made-up term for

best buds), my BFF cousin, Lola. We dressed alike and did lots of things together. I was closely acquainted with my classmates and neighbors, but my running buddy helped me decide what would occupy my time and space. We lived in very small communities and that was the format that I had been used to.

There was a time when I accepted a job as a new teacher in a small, close-knit, neighborhood school system in Arkansas at the same time I became the first black teacher to integrate that school. Segregation had been the norm. I was, of course, excited and nervous at the same time. I had just graduated from college and had very little experience; however, I was about to gain a lot in that year. I did not know exactly what to expect, but I was filled with a peace and stillness that was quickly familiar. It was all about trust—trusting oneself and trusting God.

History was being made at the same time. The Civil Rights Act of 1964 had passed and been signed into law. Southern white schools were not willing to accept this new norm, so they forced the hand of the federal government to set guidelines for school integration. I became the patsy, the token black, and the chosen trailblazer. I had to prove that the law was in effect, to a paltry degree, in our school corporation. It was a long and arduous progression, and I remain extremely aware of where we are today. We are unable to coexist peacefully and are just as separate in social and moral platforms today as we were in 1964.

I made sure, on the first day of my assignment, that I was on time and professionally clad to affirm this new cause. "*Let's do this!*" I heard myself mutter under my breath! As I entered the building with my six-year-old son, Andre, in tow, a little white boy, around seven or eight years old, zoomed up from behind us and came running like a whirlwind in a tunnel.

He passed us, screaming toward every door along the long hallway, "Hey everybody, we got a nigger teacher!"

And again, just in case no one heard him the first time, "We got a nigger teacher!"

I smiled a smile that really caused me to chuckle inside. *Did he think he was the only one to call me a nigger?* I was used to that one. I proceeded to my dugout of a room to perform my duties as the elementary school librarian. I was the test case, an appeasement of the school district to the state. They'd hired a black teacher in order to meet the mandated quota for the first phase of integration. This would be the first stage of toppling the *status quo* in the South!

Friendships were about to be tested! Fast forward to my time spent as the first black elementary teacher vs. librarian at the elementary school. The best friend I made there in my first year was the very same little boy who had called me "nigger" on my first day at the school. He would give up some of his outside play time whenever I had yard duty to hang out with me and talk "kid" stuff. He could've been out on the field, playing with his buddies, but he kept company with me until the bell rang. He was beginning to see me as a person who shared the same human qualities as he, himself. His temporary prejudice had been learned. I did not second-guess him, didn't give him the "side eye," did not accuse him, nor did I judge his parents. I was the product of what I had been taught, and that was to *love one another* and to love my enemies as much as I loved myself. God loved me enough that He allowed a spillage of His love to fall on me, so that I could love others. He has commanded it! This is the awesomeness of life when we grasp the meaning of His unconditional love.

This little guy became a friend to me. He would pick wild dandelion flowers and bring them to me. When it was his class's turn to come to the library, he brought me an apple from his packed lunch. He was quite a chatty little kid, and he was always talking to me in a way that showed a 180-degree turnaround from the first day I had encountered him. It was cool how neither he nor I ever brought up the subject of our beginning. He'd just assumed that all was well, and it was!

When you demonstrate the love of God toward others, they can see an unexplainable mark of your goodwill as you bring the glory to God in your actions! First, I needed to forgive because it was required of me. I needed to demonstrate the God-given deposits of His love in me. I needed to show myself to be open and friendly, as Jesus is a friend to me. I desired to use what my daddy gave me for the benefit of helping others and to perpetually realize His goodness toward us all. What a friend we have in Jesus! He is "a friend that sticketh closer than a brother" (Prov. 18:24 KJV). Friendship is incredibly important to Him as we see in John 15 " Greater love hath no man than this, that a man lay down his life for his friends" (John 15:13 KJV).

We can all learn lessons from little children. They come innocently into this world and can, unfortunately, become quickly tainted by what their environment feeds them. Let us strive to be as little children as in Matthew 18 where Jesus said, "unless you change and become like little children, you will never enter the kingdom of heaven. Therefore, whoever takes the lowly position of this child is the greatest in the kingdom of heaven" (Matt. 18:3–4 NIV).

God's Homework: We all have come a little short in our forgiveness of a hurtful word or something said against us. Choose to forgive now. Be the big-hearted person. Forgive someone who has hurt you and reach out and touch someone in this very special way.

9

Friendship

~⚮~

SHELLEY M. FISHER, PH.D.

A friend loves at all times, and a brother is born for adversity.
(Prov. 17:17 NKJV)

Friendships are found everywhere, but what are they really? Each of us has our own definitions. I think of my high school friend, Mary. Our families had moved into a section of the city in which the school was being integrated. We were both new neighbors and classmates.

It was not surprising when the history teacher told our class, "The neighborhood was good until 'you people' came here."

After his class, we chuckled at the negative comments. We often had laughing spells when nothing was funny. In retrospect, I recognize our silliness may have been a defense mechanism.

After high school Mary married and I went to college. We were determined to remain friends. I was her daughter's godmother. Her daughter was the flower girl in my wedding. And then, quite abruptly, Mary became suddenly ill and died at the age of twenty-seven. Of course, my grief was huge, but I continue to appreciate her participation in my first truly abiding friendship.

Throughout the years, there have been associates, people that we encounter in passing. Then there have been instances when the passing was interrupted for friendship. Those friendships evolved after work—stopping by the club to have a drink or playing bridge.

I played bridge with the same ladies for seven years. These friendships contained a genuineness. There was an "I have your back" kind of thing.

Eventually, I arrived at the spiritual awakening stage of my life. My background was traditional Baptist, yet I remained in a sense of "wow" for months as I watched individuals operate in the spiritual gifts. I soon learned of the power of God and I began to operate in my own God-given gifts. It was about this time when I noticed a pattern of human behavior that did not always align with the Word of God.

For example, one person at the workplace would change conversation styles when speaking with one person to another, sprinkling in cursing and other spicy retorts for some and not others. People are not perfect, but experiences like this can teach us the differences between a true relationship with God rather than pretense.

There were two occasions when I felt led by God to stay close and minister to two friends who were both going through divorces. In one case, I would wake up at about 3:00 A.M. and feel an overwhelming urge to call one of them. I found she always needed encouraging words at that time of the night. She was strong in her relationship with God but needed support while going through a difficult time.

With my other friend, I listened. Sometimes an open ear and a quiet mouth are the best resources you supply for a friend going through a difficult situation. I heard about the good times, the memories, and when the bad times started. I allowed her to "talk it out" without interfering and interjecting my opinion. She needed me to be an unbiased listener. Afterwards, I offered prayer.

Discernment requires looking beyond the surface into the depths of a person's heart. I believe our friendships, along with others who cross our paths, are ordained by God. There is something for us to glean from their situations. What is really happening when we allow someone to control us? What are our deficits? What is inside us that needs human validation? The solutions almost always point inward, and it is rare that we can blame anyone else.

We must develop certain personal boundaries. If people do not accept us, if they cannot celebrate our successes when God is opening new doors, we can learn to get over it. You can "shake the dust off your feet" (Matt. 10:14) and move on. We do not need to belabor the point and try to figure out why a friendship or other relationship is fading away. Our season is up with them. God has other relationships waiting for us. They simply do not fit through the door that God is opening for us.

In our prayer time, we can ask God to send us the friends He wants us to have. We do not need to be in a situation where a person is using buttery words but has a drawn sword behind his/her back. Bishop T.D. Jakes said: "People fall in love with who you are not; when they see who you really are, they feel betrayed." This is a spiritual battle. Satan wants to stop us from moving forward and growing into our next levels. He works through people to impede us. We are told in First Peter that we have an adversary who goes about as a roaring lion, seeking whom he may devour (1 Peter 5:8 author's paraphrase). You also have a heavenly Father who has a perfect plan for your life: "For I know the plans I have for you declares the Lord plans to prosper you and not to harm you, plans to give you hope and a future" (Jer. 29:11 NIV).

In the Bible, Jonathan and David were knit together. In 1 Sam. 20:41, a biblical model of friendship is portrayed. David and Jonathan, the son of King Saul, made a covenant:

> The Lord God of Israel is my witness! When I have sounded out my father sometime tomorrow, or the third day, and indeed there is good toward David, and I do not send to you and tell you may the Lord do so much more to Jonathan. But if it pleases my father to do you evil, then I will report to you and

send you away, that you may go to safety. And the Lord be with you as he has been with my father. And you shall not only show me the kindness of the Lord while I still live, that I may not die, but you shall not cut off your kindness from my house forever, no, not when the Lord has cut off every one of the enemies of David from the face of the earth. So, Jonathan made a covenant with the house of David, saying "Let the Lord require it at the hand of David's enemies." (1 Sam. 20:12–16 NKJV)

David questioned why Jonathan's father, King Saul, would want to kill him, asking, "What have I done? What is my iniquity?"

Jonathan responded in friendship, saying, "If it pleases my father to do you evil, I will tell you."

Both King Saul and his son, Jonathan, were eventually killed in battle. David and his men wept and mourned. Later on, David sought to find someone from King Saul's house to bless and show kindness for Jonathan's sake. He found Mephibosheth, the son of Jonathan, who was lame. David welcomed him at his table and treated him like one of his own sons.

In the Book of Proverbs the Bible says that Jesus is a friend who sticks closer than a brother. We may claim to have many friends, but do they stick with us in times of trouble? When we leave the doors of the church, how do our friends behave in other settings? The Message Bible puts it this way: "Friends come, and friends go, but a true friend sticks by you like family" (Prov. 18:24 NKJV).

Proverbs has many descriptive passages that include friendship:

- Wisdom is called a friend (Prov. 7:4).
- A friend loves at all times (Prov. 17:17).
- A poor man is deserted by his friends (Prov. 19:4).
- Everyone is a friend to a man who gives gifts (Prov. 19:6).

- A person with gracious speech has the king as his friend (Prov. 22:11).
- Faithful are the wounds of a friend (Prov. 27:6).
- The sweetness of a friend comes from his earnest counsel (Prov. 27:9).
- Do not forsake your father's friend (Prov. 27:10).

Inside the verses above, we can see that there are essentially two kinds of friends. One who exists because you have some material thing or possibly an association that enhances popularity. The other exists out of true love. We can use discernment and ask the Lord to send the appropriate people into our lives. It's important to note that without practicing discernment, we also run the risk of becoming the unreliable friend who brings others to ruin.

It is possible we will also make mistakes by allowing someone into our space, only to find out that they simply want to use our gifts or connections. It is relatively common to have been "burned" a time or two by such self-serving "friends." These experiences serve to remind us to be a bit more discerning and diligent and to pray before getting involved again. By studying the Word and having a consistent prayer life, we can learn to distinguish the buttery words and drawn swords. Proverbs 12 says this: "The righteous should choose his friends carefully, but the way of the wicked leads them astray" (Prov. 12:26 NKJV).

The Bible tells us to pray for our enemies, and for those who spitefully use us. This is sometimes easier said than done. But the purpose behind praying for them is to free ourselves from anger and resentment. We must learn to forgive and let the past go. We should not beat ourselves up because we did not see the betrayal coming. We can shake the dust off our feet and move on in our development. In the Bible, Peter says, "Think it not strange when the fiery trials come to try you…" (1 Peter 4:12 NKJV). We can always stay connected to God—the friend who sticks closer than a brother—and He will see us through.

Finally, we can expect there to be times in our lives when God will prune and cut away friendships that are not conducive to where He is trying to take us. Some relationships may have a short-term lifespan from the beginning. Only God knows when they are no longer needed. When this happens, we should not try to hang on to what God is loosening. He may reveal the details to us by His Spirit. To be able to recognize His Voice we must study and know the Word and have a diligent prayer life. This way, we can submit to God's perfect plan for our lives.

We are all at different places on our spiritual journeys. God sends Christian friends, who he has previously ordained, to help us get to the next level. These friends are valuable assets provided to accompany us along the journey. At a time during my spiritual growth (or, maybe *upheaval* is more appropriate), I began to question some of the practices in my denomination. I had an unrest in my spirit and wanted more of the God that I had read about in the Bible. The Lord sent an older gentleman in my life who was not of my denomination. He taught and mentored me, explaining the unrest was due to spiritual growth. The Bible says: "Every purpose is established by counsel; but only with good advice make war" (Prov. 20:18 KJV). We never know who the Lord will thrust across our path to bless and counsel us in the ways we should go, but we can remain true to His instructions as we navigate friendships.

God's Homework: Does your personal definition of friendship align with God's Word? What characteristics do you possess that make a good friend? Make a list of qualities that you can incorporate to become a better friend. Ask the Lord to send the appropriate friend into your life and allow Him to select your friends. He ordains those who cross your path to guide you to your destiny.

Supernaturally So

10

The Visits

❧

SHELLEY M. FISHER, PH.D.

*Do not forget to entertain strangers, for by so doing some
have unwittingly entertained angels.* (Heb. 13:2 NKJV)

I taught in an inner-city elementary school. The high school was
nearby. Often former students would come by to say hello. On
one occasion a teenager I'd taught in the fifth grade (and who was
now in tenth) came by the school to deliver distressing news. She
announced she had been diagnosed as an alcoholic and was about
to be admitted to the "psych" ward at a local hospital. She asked
me if I would come to see her. I was not in ministry at the time,
nor did I have any counseling skills; however, I felt compelled to
say yes.

The first time I went to see Joanie (not her real name), I had
to pass through double iron doors under heavy security. After
reaching the patient ward, I had to go down a hall and speak to
someone inside a cage, built with heavy bars, to make my visit
request. I was given directions to a waiting room, which was decid-
edly more pleasant and furnished with several sofas and tables lit-
tered with magazines. It was there I would wait for Joanie.

When Joanie finally arrived, she was glad to see me. She
admitted that she was not sure I would come to visit. I let her
know I wanted to do what I could to help her. The first two visits
were uneventful, but by the third visit, Joanie blamed everyone in

her life for her condition. She also spoke of harming herself. My response was to suggest she take responsibility for her actions. I felt uncomfortable about this and extremely ill-equipped.

I went to my then pastor, lamenting my involvement with Joanie and asking him for advice. He told me he did not let people worry him. He said he would ignore her. This did not register well with me.

On my next visit, I thought I had garnered the resolve to tell Joanie I could not help her and I was not planning to come and see her again. This time when I arrived on the ward it was quiet. The lady behind the cage said the patients were in a craft class, but I could have a seat and wait. I went into the waiting room and sat down, mentally rehearsing what I would say to Joanie. Then a nurse came in and sat down beside me. She was dressed in white from head to toe. She greeted me, asking how I was doing. I unexpectedly spilled my feelings all over her. I told her about my insecurity and general helplessness. I explained about advising Joanie to accept responsibility for her actions. The nurse was warm and understanding. I felt as though I had known her forever; she spoke with such wisdom and authority. She soothed my fears by telling me to keep doing what I was doing. She reiterated that it was good to tell Joanie to accept responsibility. She said I was doing the right thing and to continue to support her. The nurse was so kind, and she "refueled" me to deal with Joanie. Shortly after she left, Joanie came back from art class.

We had a pleasant visit. Joanie was smiling and happy. We reflected on some of the students who had been in her class. The visit was refreshing. I told her I would come to visit her again the following week.

I felt confident when I visited Joanie the next week. The patients were returning from their art class and again I was told to sit in the waiting room. I thought of the nurse who had helped to assuage my fears. I went down the hall and asked the lady behind the cage if I could talk to the nurse I had spoken with last week. I wanted to thank her.

The lady behind the cage said, "There are no nurses here."

I said, "Yes, there was the one with blonde hair who visited with me in the waiting room last week."

The lady added, "There is no one like that who works here. There are no nurses on this unit."

My thoughts ran rampant! *Could I have been talking to an angel?* I could only think of the Scripture that says, "Do not forget to entertain strangers for by so doing some have unwittingly entertained angels" (Heb. 13:2 NKJV).

God's Homework: God is mindful of everything that concerns you. When you acknowledge Him, seek His guidance, and speak His Word, you dispatch angels to come to your aid. Can you think of a time when something happened to you that was "unexplainable?" Could it have been the angelic host of heaven? Remain open to receive from God in unconventional ways. Study God's Word to know His voice and to recognize His interventions.

11

A Supernatural Appearance

⟨✦⟩

ERNESTINE MEADOWS MAY

*Be not forgetful to entertain strangers; for thereby some
have entertained angels unawares.* (Heb 13:2 KJV)

It was not unusual to gather together with friends to go on a
shopping trip to find a few things we needed for our home. I
was the driver and, of course, I need to make sure I had sufficient
gas. While at the service station, I asked the attendant to check
the oil because the car had been using a lot recently.

We left laughing, talking, and having great fun. Each of us
knew what we were looking to purchase. Now, the balance of this
story may be told by each of us in a completely different way. I
already know that the Holy Spirit has my eye and ear and, to my
way of thinking, works in ways that are totally out of the ordinary.

Somewhere on I-94, between 115th Street and 111th Street,
my car began to accelerate out of control—even with my foot
removed from the pedal. I quickly accelerated to a speed of 98
miles per hour! I didn't know what to do. Everything happened
so fast. My mind was racing as the car sped under its own power
down the road. I heard prayers from inside the car. Once again, I
applied my foot on the brake, as the car had revved up to about
110 miles per hour.

I whispered a prayer to myself, "Oh Lord, help me!"

I tried downshifting the gears, but it didn't slow the car. I thought to turn the key to the Off position but then I remembered right after that someone had once told me to never turn the key off when an automatic transmission car is in motion. Turning it off would lock the gear shift and the steering wheel and it would be extremely hard to steer afterwards.

The 111th Street exit was closed. I knew I had to get off of the expressway. Thankfully, God had already cleared the highway. I don't remember seeing any cars in or around my path. I was able to head for the exit and thought this might be a good time to turn the key to the Off position. The car rolled to a stop. We were all astonished. We all got out of the car and tried to sort out what we had just experienced.

From absolutely nowhere, three young men in jeans and plaid shirts appeared. Without saying a word, they went about their assignment. There was no car visible that they could have driven to our location. One of the three quietly popped the hood and looked underneath. It seemed as if everyone was moving inside a haze of thin smoke, as though I was watching a movie. Another of the young men walked away from the car, looking down on the side of the exit in the grassy areas where the car had traveled. The third surveyed the perimeter at the 111th Street exit as though they were looking for something that had been lost. One of the young men came back toward the car holding something in his hands. As he drew closer, I could see that it was the oil cap to the car.

Now, I can't remember how this was known to me, but the problem was that the oil cap had fallen off and lodged itself in the throttle linkage, jamming it wide open and causing great accelera-tion. The car had revved so that no amount of braking could stop it, nor was I able to properly shift gears. The serviceman who had checked the oil evidently had not put the cap on tightly enough, potentially setting the stage for a possibly fatal accident. But what the enemy had meant for evil, God used as a connection to the supernatural, creating a miracle.

Our visitors had moved about as though everything they did was divinely orchestrated. They went about putting everything back into its proper place within the automobile. The hood went down and as quickly as they had appeared, they left, without us seeing which way they went. Who were the visitors? Angels in blue jeans and plaid shirts! I tell you God has angelic mechanics ready to help us in times of need. You've probably heard the phrase, "God's got this!" This is the definition of what that means. There was no evidence that they had ever been there, except the etching they left on my heart and mind forever. It can only happen in the supernatural!

The other ladies may remember a different version of this event. We certainly could have had a totally different ending; however, the script was written by His Grace. I am reminded of two verses when I think of this harrowing event. First, "Thou wilt keep him in perfect peace, whose mind is stayed on thee: because he trusts in you" (Isa. 26:3 KJV) and also, "Be not forgetful to entertain strangers; for thereby some have entertained angels unawares" (Heb. 13:2 KJV).

God's Homework: Write a short statement about a time that you are sure than an occurrence in your life had to do with God's divine plan of intervention, in other words, a time when God showed up in your defense.

12

Be Still and Know

✺

GLORIA SHARPE SMITH

During the night an Angel of the Lord opened the door . . .
(Acts 5:19 NIV)

Have you ever had an experience that left you wondering *"what just happened?"* or sat quietly and allowed a thought to enter your mind and question the possibility of it becoming reality? These experiences happen you know, and when they do, oftentimes we tuck them away without any fanfare or, maybe, we casually mention them to a friend at a time that seems appropriate. Such phenomena are usually thought of as mystic or intuitional.

Have you ever longed for an encounter with God where you just wanted to know, without any doubt, that you're personally known by Him and that He really performs miracles? It's not uncommon to have these desires. There's security and confidence in having this kind of relationship with Him.

I've gained a closer relationship and a deeper faith with Him as my spiritual life continues to grow and be strengthened. My walk with God is a supernatural walk of faith with the Divine. For example, one evening while sitting on the sofa and looking out of the window as barrels of rain poured from the sky and lightning bolts ripped through the air, I had this thought: *"Can lightning come inside of the house and strike something?"* Shortly, I heard a loud clap of thunder, and the chime of my doorbell gave a loud ring. I couldn't believe it. *"Wow, Lord. You just answered my question!"* I thought to myself. The sound from the doorbell had been set off by the lightning. No one was at the front door to manually activate the bell from the outside. The box that contained the chime for the bell was located high on a wall upstairs. The ceilings were twenty feet high, and the bell was close to the top. I was downstairs and looked up at the chime box as it rang out.

This was not some far-out, spooky, mystical event; it was a supernatural encounter afforded me to experience the power and capability of God. My belief and faith were enhanced by this experience. I've learned that God cares about everything that concerns us. His intention is for everyone to know Him personally. He wants you to know Him and to know that He knows you better than you know yourself. He knows how to reveal Himself in ways that are unique to your likening. He wants you to know with confidence that you have a relationship with Him. Thus, He's a master at arranging personalized encounters.

On another occasion, I remember preparing for a Zoom meeting and paying attention to every detail involved by putting my two miniature pinschers in their play area for quiet time during my meeting. I followed the routine by getting their snack from the canister and walking to the bedroom, with the pups jumping for joy as we went. They love the treats and my Zoom time for that very reason. Once they were in the room, I gave them their treats and told them to have a nice nap and that I would see them in a while. I walked out of the room and closed the door. I could hear it catch as it closed shut.

The two-hour meeting was intense, and I was fully engaged. Several times, I heard the girls barking, which wasn't unusual when they wanted attention or needed to go out. I ignored them but was mindful that as soon as the meeting was over, I had to attend to them. Finally, the meeting ended and as soon as it did, the phone rang. I answered and the conversation lasted for a time that was not agreeable with the girls. They were barking so loudly that the person on the phone heard them and asked if there was a problem with Melody and Reign. I quickly told her that I had just finished a two-hour meeting and they were ready to go out. We continued our conversation for a while longer, when suddenly the call dropped, and the conversation was over. I didn't try to call my friend back but determined that it was time to give the girls some attention. However, before doing so, I went into another room and sat down. The barking had ceased, and all was well. The door to the room where I was sitting was open and there was no one else in the house with me. It was just Melody, Reign, and me. I could see out into another room of the house when suddenly, it was as if a gentle flow of air entered the room. It was quiet and nothing unusual was going on when in walks both Melody and Reign. They were stretching like they had just awakened from a long nap. I was in total amazement to see them and to realize that I had not even heard the sound of their tags jingling from their collars as they came from the bedroom where I had left them. "How did you get out of the bedroom? Who opened the door?" I asked the questions knowing that the dogs couldn't answer, and I really wasn't expecting them to. It was supernatural.

I know that there was no way possible for them to get out of the room without someone opening the door and I didn't do it! *"Amazing,"* I thought. They came looking for me and I didn't make a sound. I was dumbfounded. Then I remembered, earlier that morning, during my devotional time, I had prayed a simple prayer that went something like this: "Lord, I want to have a supernatural experience with you, but nothing spooky or scarry. You know me, and you know my heart. You know what will work for me and I trust you." That was it, and I proceeded to go on with my day. It wasn't until I was staring at the girls and asking God, "How did they get out of the bedroom?" then I realized my simple prayer was answered. God had spoken to my spirit.

Okay, Lord, I believe that you sent an angel to open the bedroom door for them so that their needs could be met and my simple prayer request could be answered. The incident did not cause me any fear or uneasiness; actually, it was serene. There was a deep sense of fulfillment in my spirit which left me knowing that there's peace in the presence of God. He knows how to personalize our experiences with Him so that all doubt and fear is erased.

I also had witnessed my girls' demeanor change because of their supernatural experience. I believe an angel was sent to open the door for them so that they could get to me to have their needs met. They walked quietly into the room, and somehow, they looked differently, almost sleepy, if there is such a thing. Melody did a long stretch as if she was recovering from a long nap. Her demeanor was different in a calm and serene manner. This was very unusual for her (as she is more of a barker and the attention seeker between the two). For the remainder of the day and well into the evening, they were different. It was supernatural.

This encounter reminded me of the Bible story in Acts 5:19 that tells of prison doors being opened supernaturally by angels. My dogs were released from the bedroom by angels because I asked God to give me a supernatural experience that would not spook me but one that I would know was from Him just for me. He answered that simple prayer and He'll do the same for you.

God's Homework: Ask God to reveal Himself to you in a new way that leaves no doubt in your mind that He is with you.

13

The Supernatural in the Principal's Office

⟡

SHELLEY M. FISHER, PH.D.

"Not by might nor by power, but by my Spirit,"
says the LORD of hosts. (Zech. 4:6 NKJV)

It was a brisk autumn morning. The children entered the building with laughter and fall colored leaves attached to their feet. Mrs. Jones and I stood watching the children and talked of plans for the day. Then, our gaze fell upon Ms. Smith coming down the walk in her bulwark, six-foot frame, her coat flying from side to side. She was obviously approaching us and looking as though she had been chewing nails.

I looked to Mrs. Jones for an explanation. Bobby (not his real name), Ms. Smith's son, was in her class. Mrs. Jones had complained about her son not having his homework. Belatedly, I reminded Mrs. Jones about our agreement that we would not contact Ms. Smith about Bobby. We had him under observation because he was always hitting the other students. Our social worker, along with Mrs. Jones and I, had come to the consensus that someone at home was probably hitting him. I quickly told Mrs. Jones to follow my lead in dealing with Ms. Smith.   M s . Smith angrily announced she needed to take Bobby home. She looked irritated and distraught. Mrs. Jones began to talk about Bobby's positive behavior and work. Ms. Smith was not buying it. She simply restated that she had come to get him to take him home.

"And I want him now."

I intervened and told Ms. Smith that Bobby's class was taking a test. The test was mandatory. It was important that he be in school. She paused and listened. I ushered the three of us toward Mrs. Jones's classroom and told her to get the test ready. I found a large chair and set it in front of a window facing the classroom, so Ms. Smith could see us. Her eyes were still red and fiery. She was still breathing heavily.

Each grade level administers a diagnostic principal's test twice per semester. I instructed Mrs. Jones to get me the tests.

Under my breath, I was praying, "Lord show me how to deal with this. How do I defuse Ms. Smith? I did not have any proof to call the police or protective services about anything; besides, I would be breaching the trust with the school and with Ms. Smith and Bobby. I proceeded to administer the test with the first graders, reading each item aloud. Mrs. Jones walked around the room monitoring the students and all the while, Ms. Smith glared at us through the window. I asked Mrs. Jones to go to the intercom and call my administrative assistant.

When she arrived, I gave the test responsibilities to Mrs. Jones while I talked with the administrative assistant. I asked her to summon the only male person in the building and requested that he sit in my office in the chair next to my desk. He was a talker, so I added instructions that he was not to utter a word. He was just to sit there. I knew the situation was volatile and I was trying to prevent things from getting out of hand.

I still had not heard from God. Ms. Smith was beginning to shift from side to side in the chair. We had engaged the first-grade students for twenty-five minutes without a break. I knew I had to act soon, but I did not have a clue as to what to do. God was not saying anything to me. I could not allow Ms. Smith to take Bobby home. She looked too unstable.

At this point, I left the room and asked that Ms. Smith enter my office. I told her the children were almost finished with the test. She was compliant. As we walked in my office, the male teacher was positioned in the chair next to my desk. I ushered Ms. Smith to a seat at the conference table.

After that, I begin to walk, pace, and pray, saying, "Father, in the name of Jesus . . .."

Whatever the Holy Spirit spoke to me I prayed loudly as I paced in front of my desk. I do not know how long this went on. I was fervently petitioning the Father to intervene on behalf of Ms. Smith.

Then suddenly, I heard a loud shrill shriek come from Ms. Smith; next, I heard sobbing. She cried out as though her insides were being wrenched, as though her innermost organs were being torn from her body. I stopped and stood perfectly still. She cried and cried. The male teacher's eyes were as big as saucers. I motioned to him to control his facial expressions. We quietly stood by while Ms. Smith released her pain through her sobs.

Finally, she stopped. I handed Ms. Smith a box of tissues. Her countenance had been transformed to allowing a smile to dance upon her face. I was relieved and thankful to God.

When she finally spoke, she calmly said, "Thank you. I am going to take Bobby home, but I assure you he will be at school tomorrow. Thank you."

God had answered the prayer and poured His love out on Ms. Smith. The male teacher told me he liked the way I handled the situation. I told him I had nothing to do with it and thanked him for sitting quietly next to my desk. I was only one of the vessels that God had used to get his work done within Ms. Smith that day.

Bobby was in school the next day. We were able to contact community agencies to get Ms. Smith some resources. We continued to speak frequently to Ms. Smith, now in her new position as a cashier at the local supermarket. God answers prayer. He moves supernaturally, not by power nor by might, but by His Spirit His Will is done in the earth.

God's Homework: God knows what He has put on the inside of you. Those gifts are to be used to reach out to others. It does not matter where you are or what the platform is, God will get His Will done. Yield to Him and learn to hear His voice, so that you can follow His commands to build His kingdom. Trust God to have a solution to problems.

14

What Did I Say?

∽✕∽

SHELLEY M. FISHER, PH.D.

If anyone speaks, let him speak as of the oracles of God. If anyone ministers, let him do it with the ability which God supplies, that in all things God may be glorified through Jesus Christ, to whom belong the glory and the dominion forever and ever. (1 Peter 4:11 NKJV)

"Now faith is the substance of things hoped for the evidence of things not seen" (Heb. 11:1 NKJV). If you want faith, you can pray for it. It is also likely that the Lord will give you the opportunity to test your faith. While I worked as principal at a school, I was blessed with a staff who were exceptionally hard working. Students were continually busy learning and teachers were equally busy teaching—a principal's ideal. We had good relationships within the community, test scores were soaring, and it seemed all was well. That is until I received a call from the superintendent saying she had received a petition, initiated by parents and stating they wanted me removed. I was shocked. I explained what we were doing, how progress was continually being made, how relationships were good, and, particularly, that I had not received any complaints from any parents.

I prayed about the situation, asking God to reveal what was going on. The superintendent began calling after every major successful event. One night, we had a family fun night, and 450 parents out of 500 enrolled students had been in attendance. The next morning, I received another call from our central office. This upper-level management behavior became quite puzzling, but I chose not to talk with anybody about it. I did not even mention it to my husband.

When the superintendent sent me a copy of the petition, I pulled one teacher aside. I knew that she was someone I could trust not to create a hornet's nest of gossip. She had been at the school for years. After examining the document, she informed me that the parents who had signed it did not have students in the school anymore. They were the parents of students who had gone on to middle and high school. She started to exit my office, then turned to mention that she had seen some of the parents listed on the petition dropping students off in the front of the building during the morning hours.

I kept a quiet stance, believing God would expose and rectify the situation. One day during lunch hour, I was standing with two parents—one a paid employee—in the lunchroom, a female parent whose daughter was in second grade and a grandfather whose grandson was in sixth grade. I turned to them and what came out of my mouth shocked me.

I said, "You are the ones circulating the petition."

The female gasped.

The grandfather said, "She started that petition and had me sign it. I did not want to, because I think you are doing a good job. When the parents came in the morning, dropping off neighborhood kids, we got signatures. Their children do not even attend this school."

The female spun around, heading toward the door and saying, "I'm *outta* here."

This woman worked with the student council and assisted with selling candy. Some of the money over which she was responsible was missing. I was forced to have a conference with her concerning the matter. She returned about a third of the money. I reassigned her to lunchroom duty. This, I believe, was her motivation for the phony petition. After two months passed, she never came back to the school or called to report her intentions. Finally, the superintendent called and said she would terminate the woman for abandoning her post.

That is what faith will do when you rest in Him. I could have phoned my colleagues, spilled the story, and lamented my woes: *What am I going to do?* Instead, I put it in God's hands and He solved the problem.

God's Homework: When you do not know what to do or what to say, God will put words in your mouth. He gives solutions to problems when you trust Him. Do not fret about the situation, just take it to God who already has the answer. Position yourself to receive from Him.

15

The Hounds of Hell Shall Not Prevail

❧

ERNESTINE MEADOWS MAY

For the Lord does not see as man sees; for man looks at the outward appearance, but the Lord looks at the heart. (1 Sam. 16:7 ESV)

"You don't know me. I've only allowed you to know who you think I am, says me!" We can all attest to this statement. We may claim to be transparent, but woe be unto us all if we were. I have been discovering "me" since as far back as I can remember. I've hidden some thoughts, deeds, and ramblings, just as you probably have. Who is perfect? Who carries the greatest sin? Here I am, Lord. You know me from the inside out. Thank You that You know my heart!

Additionally, I choose to be a vessel. If He chooses to use me, I am available. I am more than amazed as I've come to understand how an ordinary person on a journey through a land can be set to a purpose orchestrated by the Will of God. I am not privy to all of the answers or outcomes, but I trust Him to reveal the fullness of all things *in due time.*

There was a time when I worked at an alternative home for young people. The opportunity raised in me another level of faith to operate within. I was further instilled with a belief in the supernatural by what occurred on a particular Saturday evening. The purpose of the home was to intervene for children by separating them from their home setting, for one reason or another. Whatever their issue, the students needed counseling and guidance in social and emotional behaviors from respected experts in fields of behavior modification.

I was on assigned duty, along with one of the more seasoned staff members. It was part of the protocol that there would be a male and a female team for each work shift. It was one of those days when the children, mostly teens, were wound up. It was difficult to settle them down with rhetoric. Later into the evening, they were forced to go to their dormitory rooms early because of their rudeness and disrespect concerning directives from the staff. They were not happy campers. Frustration and anger flared up from within their respectful dorms. I was asked to go into the girls dorm to get everyone settled down. The male staff member was to go into the boys dorm to do the same. On my way there, I was thinking of a strategy to use. I was the new-kid-on-the-block and I had not established myself as an *authoritative person of interest* with them.

I turned off the lights. In my spirit I was calm. I heard instructions to pull up a chair near the doorway entrance. This was the only place where there was light entering the room. Still, the noise, screaming, and nonsensical craziness echoed from the room continuously. It was time for the super to meet the natural. I felt it coming on!

In a quiet, soft voice I began to sing in the spirit a song that I didn't know in my natural language. It flowed out of my mouth in lyrically uttered tongues, as the Holy Spirit gave it. I sang with confidence and authority. I looked over at their stacked beds to see girls begin to drop their heads to their pillows, then raise themselves up in a drowsy stupor to see if they could figure out what was happening. They tried to talk, but words would not come from their mouths. Their bodies went from rigid to slumped. They were dropping into the softness of their beds *like flies!* This was awesome to my eyes. The Lord was performing His Word, as in Isaiah

43, "Behold, I will do a new thing; (said the Lord) now it shall spring forth; shall ye not know it? I will even make a way in the wilderness, and rivers in the desert" (Isa. 43:19 KJV). They were under the spell of the Holy Spirit, and just like that, the girls fell fast asleep.

I moved my chair back into its place, closed the door, and said, "Good night."

Later, as I usually do during my evening prayers, I asked of the Lord, *"What was that?"* I heard in my spirit, *"The hounds of hell shall not prevail against you!"*

Ladies and gentlemen, God dispatches His warring angels to fight against the forces of evil in our lives, when we call on His Great Name. That is as it should be, according to Isaiah 65, *"Before they call, I will answer; while they are still speaking, I will hear"* (Isa. 65:24 KJV).

Father, I pray that ears will be open to hear, eyes will be opened to see, and hearts will receive the things that you have in store for Your people when they believe. I declare and decree empowerment for the person reading this, along with their household.

In Jesus Christ. Amen.

God's Homework: If you're having difficulties in school, struggling with family life or not quite feeling your best, open your journal and write out a sentence that says:

Note to self:
I love you and will not allow myself to _____ anymore.

16

The Supernatural in the Cornfields

❧

SHELLEY M. FISHER, PH.D.

Likewise the Spirit also helps in our weaknesses. For we do not know what we should pray for as we ought, but the Spirit Himself makes intercession for us with groanings which cannot be uttered. (Rom. 8:26 NKJV)

My co-author Gloria and I were on a consulting assignment to conduct a workshop that introduced change paradigms. We were driving on a narrow two-lane highway in the southern part of our state, surrounded by cornfields on both sides as far as we could see. We rode through the cornfields, engaging in good-natured banter until suddenly, it was as if someone punched me in the pit of my stomach. I began to pray, wail, and cry out. I was speaking in tongues, struggling to keep my hands on the steering wheel. Gloria immediately began praying and crying out in tongues too, while we drove through a couple miles of cornfields.

When I finally collected myself, I realized it was the Lord speaking to me. He was letting me know that the area had a high rate of incest and that children were being abused.

We reached our destination without further incident, joined our colleagues, and took charge of our professional duties. I didn't receive confirmation of His message then, but a couple of weeks later when I met with a social worker I did. We were catching up on our current activities. I talked about having done a workshop recently and where it was. The social worker commented that her office received many complaints from the general location, primarily concerning incest and child abuse.

As Gloria and I passed through the region we were experiencing the pain and anguish of the children. God always has a plan. He looks for those who will obey Him. Praying for those children remained a part of my intercession for a while, until I was released. God needs us to be faithful to Him to achieve His will on the earth. At that time, God needed intercessors to pray for His children in that area. Gloria and I were available.

God's Homework: When you have a life of prayer, you become sensitive to the voice of God and He will download in you a need to pray, even when your intellect does not understand the situation. He is a Spirit and moves by His Spirit. The supernatural is real. Hear His voice. Yield to the Holy Spirit and pray in tongues releasing miraculous intercession for people whom we know and for those we do not know.

17

Following the Unction

❧

SHELLEY M. FISHER, PH.D.

My sheep hear My voice and I know them, and they follow Me.
(John 10:27 NKJV)

I lived within ten minutes of the school where I worked. At the time, I was teaching fifth grade. I had awakened one morning at my normal time and was going through my daily routine; however, I quite suddenly felt an overwhelming urge to leave early. I was puzzled by the thought because I had nothing outstanding or compelling that should draw me to the school.

I arrived at 6:55 A.M. The main hallway was quiet and semi-dark with only a few lights on. I waved at the principal and secretaries as I headed to the elevator and ascended to my third-floor room. There was no one stirring, not even a mouse. I set down my briefcase, hung up my coat and began going through various things on my desk. It wasn't long before I realized I was thirsty. There was a water fountain right outside of my door, but the fountain around the corner had colder water. I headed that way, turning left with the exit stairwell on my right.

As I rounded the corner, I saw a colleague. I greeted her and commented on her early arrival. She looked at me for a moment and then fell into my arms, crying uncontrollably. I asked what was wrong, she literally could not speak. I maneuvered her back into my classroom and closed the door.

She began to whimper and managed to get out the words, "My brother is molesting my niece."

Her imploring expression beckoned to me, as if she were trying to say, *"Can you help me?"* I'm sure the look on my face was announcing the seriousness of the accusation because she immediately explained; she shared certain details with me to verify that her niece was being violated by her father. She succeeded in assuring me she had proof about what was happening. She had only come to school early to leave her lesson plans. She was much too upset to work.

Now what do I do with this? I thought.

First, I asked my colleague if we could pray together. Next, I asked God for direction and to order our steps.

When our prayer was over, I said, "You know we are obligated by law to report abuse of a child. What we are going to do now is go to the principal's office, call protective services, and wait for them there."

"Okay," she said and straightened herself up.

We took the nearby stairwell down to the principal's office. When protective services arrived, the principal gave them and our colleague the use of his office for privacy.

My colleague came to my classroom before leaving the building and thanked me for being there for her. She told me that protective services would take it from there.

Even though I had no idea why I felt compelled to arrive at work early, the Holy Spirit had a plan to "set the captives free." Had I not gotten up to get water from the colder water fountain, or if I had arrived a few seconds later, my colleague would have probably continued down the stairwell. This was another *kairos* moment. It could only be defined as strategic timing—God's timing! We should not ignore the nudging of the Spirit or any intuition that we sense. God needs us to get His plan accomplished. I believe I followed His lead that morning, and I pray that our intervention may have saved that child from years of suffering.

My arrival at work constituted a mission accomplished for God who used me to help bring deliverance to a teenager. The Holy Spirit is perpetually speaking! Can you hear Him? When you hear Him, will you obey?

God's Homework: Can you hear His voice? Do you sense His urging you to take an action? Follow His voice and there is probably an assignment just around the corner. You have an unction from the Holy One to walk under His covering. Read and meditate the Word to know God's voice.

18

Working Within the Kingdom

⟶✦⟶

GLORIA SHARPE SMITH

This people have I formed for myself; they shall show forth my praise. (Isa. 43:21 KJV)

Where do I start? How do I begin to tell the story of how God called four women together for a project? There's an identity that I've embraced that defines who I am in this season of my life, along with others close to my age. We're sisters in Christ, Daughters of God, and dear friends. We love life and are retired from the day-to-day routine of a demanding career. We can breathe easily, sleep late if we choose to, and just enjoy the goodness of God and how He's blessed us to prosper and be witnesses to many of His amazing and wonderful acts of love, grace, and kindness. From time to time, He has also blessed us to see displays of His mighty power. For instance, when I ministered in one of the worship services in Saransk, Russia, I saw with my own eyes, the left leg of a young boy lengthened to become the same length as his right leg. When he initially sat in a chair with both of his legs extended, it was obvious that his left leg was shorter. His desire was to walk without a limp. In his own words, in the form of a prayer request, he asked for God to mend his leg so that he could "walk better." By faith, we laid hands on him and prayed for God to lengthen the shorter leg and He did!

Experiences such as this have occurred throughout the years. God has been steadily depositing stories and experiences into my life. So why would I think that He wouldn't call on me for a withdrawal?

It was not unusual for me to have fairly frequent conversations via telephone with my friend, Doretha, since I had moved to Texas. She was still in Indiana. This was our way of keeping in touch to pray for whatever concerns there may have been. I was also eager to know how things were going in Gary. After all, I had lived in Indiana for over thirty years.

I was certain of one thing. During the pandemic, I could always call her, knowing that she would be at home. Admittedly, it has not always been the same for her concerning me. Occasionally, I wasn't at home when she called, but my cell phone was always handy. I would answer and make a promise to call her back. That is exactly what happened during a late afternoon chat in August 2020. The conversation began with the usual small talk. One thing led to another. We always managed to share some experiences that we called a "But God" moment. We were both watching television daily and seeing long lines of people who were out of work and low on food. We expressed compassion and began to reflect on the blessed lives that we've been afforded. Oftentimes Doretha would say something like, "That's a book."

I would respond, "Maybe someday."

As I was telling her about what I was seeing on my TV, an overwhelming desire came upon me to tell the world that not everyone was having the same experience during the pandemic. I knew of no one who was hungry or out of work: "But God!" I felt the need to brag on Him and His faithfulness to me through the years. Then, this small, still voice arose in my spirit that said, "*You, and other women that you know, are blessed and have hundreds of stories and testimonies that you can tell.*" I felt compelled by the Spirit of God to contact Shelley Fisher and Ernestine May. Mind you, these sisters were not on my regular call list, although we could initiate a conversation at any given time and connect. Our spirits just always seemed to stay connected.

But this was different. Shelley and Ernestine are both published writers and I've never written a book. I told Doretha Rouse, who I was conversing with, what I had heard and what was on my mind, and that I believed God had said to include her. She agreed.

"The four of us are to write a book of stories and testimonies about God's faithfulness, grace, and love for his people." I said, "Between us, there are hundreds of true-life stories that can be told that would strengthen someone's faith and give them hope, and most of all, show them how God consistently answers prayer."

Before getting off the phone with Doretha, I volunteered to contact Ernestine and Shelley.

My first thought was to create an anthology that would highlight stories regarding our years as educators and our work with children. Then, there were the thoughts of young women who might benefit. We would essentially be following the injunction in Titus 2:

> Similarly, teach the older women to live in a way
> that honor God. They must not slander others or be
> heavy drinkers. Instead, they should teach others
> what is good. These older women must train the
> younger women to love their husbands and their
> children to live wisely and be pure, to work in their
> homes, to do good, and to be submissive to their
> husbands. They will not bring shame on the word
> of God. (Titus 2:3–5 NLT)

Many years of married life, our own adult children and grands qualify us to stand in this arena. Needless to say, I invited my sisters to join me on a Zoom call to reconnect and share what had been impressed on my heart. The approach was simple and enthusiastic because we are of one spirit. Both of my sisters responded positively and wanted to know how soon to get started. I told my sisters the call to fast and pray for guidance was the next step. We know that God rewards obedience, so following through was not difficult. Ernestine sent a text message the next day that suggested a name for the project. Meanwhile, I was wondering how to participate in writing a book with experienced authors, asking myself: *What's my writer's niche? What's my voice?* All of these questions were racing in my head while my heart was saying, *"Just brag on God. You can trust Him."* I could easily do that.

Believing in and trusting God, for me, is a way of life. It began years ago when my grandmother offered me the best piece of advice ever, by saying simply, "Gloria Jean, just trust in the Lord."

My peace and confidence come from this familiar place. Life has presented me with many opportunities to strengthen my faith, primarily because I stand on verses like: "Finally, my brethren, be strong in the Lord and in the power of his might" (Eph. 6:10 NKJV).

The fact that God is faithful and can be trusted is a true life lesson. Situations may not always work out the way that I expect them to, but they always work out for my good. Sometimes it's difficult to know exactly what to do in a situation or how to respond to someone about a particular concern or issue. For example, when my sisters and I began tossing around titles for the book, I felt very strongly about a title that appealed to me. I thought it would be perfect, though the rest of the group did not agree. We spent hours discussing the matter and speaking up for our favorites. I felt I was not being heard, but I knew I could trust God to bring us into agreement on a title of His choosing in due time. Therefore, I agreed on a title that I didn't particularly like. My prayer was, *"Lord, You know my thoughts about the title and if You're okay with it, I'm okay. But please, change it if it's not what You want it to be. Let there be honest agreement."*

Our book had one title for about five weeks. During that period, I remained hopeful that we could find a title change on which everyone would agree. Insisting on my chosen title was *not* going to be my action of choice. Instead, I was *actively* choosing to trust God in prayer. He did not disappoint me.

Early one Tuesday morning, Ernestine sent us a text message that contained a beautifully scripted, "Sisters of the Gift." There it was. I knew immediately that we had the title for "His brag book," divinely selected by Him for His glory.

Shelley responded, "Wow! Sounds like the title to me."

My response was, "That's prophetic. The book is in the making, along with the gift of sisterhood. Hey! We've got it going on. Thank you, Jesus!"

It was time for me to do the happy dance. Just like that, my peace and my faith had been strengthened and, once again, rewarded. We were all in agreement about the title.

Now the stories that we've decided to share make perfect sense. We intend to proclaim that Jesus is the ultimate gift. We believe He has chosen to present Himself to our readers through our experiences. During the pandemic, I'm not only surviving, but thriving. I'm enjoying a newfound relationship with my sisters. We have formed a business and gotten closer through our weekly meetings and storytelling sessions. My memory has been challenged and proven to be a valuable asset. At the beginning of this work, I didn't realize fully just how much living I've been blessed to do. My life is full and there are many more stories to tell. I'll also concentrate on enjoying those of my sisters, because indeed, they are a gift to me. We are eager for God to call upon us to share the gift.

God's Homework: Is God calling you to interact with others concerning a project that He needs completed? Step up and take it on—by reaching out to your "team members" today.

19

Eyewitness to His Majesty

✧

ERNESTINE MEADOWS MAY

*[T]he gospel unto you with the Holy Ghost sent
down from heaven; which things the angels
desire to look into.* (1 Peter 1:12 KJV)

Hallelujah! is the greatest premier praise to God. What would beckon heaven's angels to earth to inquire of things not experienced in their holy habitat? Many of us desire to know what heaven is like. We visualize that great mansion that Jesus said He is going to prepare for us when He comes again. We ponder what will happen when He receives us unto Himself, that where He is we shall also dwell (John 14:3). The mansion is described as a brilliance of the glory of God and that of jasper, clear as crystal, with streets paved with clear gold (Rev. 21:11). The angels desire to know the salvation of God on the earth.

Let us not lose sight of heavenly things, for surely, these things from earth are temporary and shall all pass away someday. We will not go to the grave to become rot, ash, fodder for earthworms, but we shall live in the house of the Lord, forever—our home of choice! God has not abandoned us. The body of Christ is alive and well. We are the church. We come together in full obedience to the Word of God that compels us to not forsake the assembling of ourselves together—exhorting one another and so much more—as we see the day approaching (Heb. 10:25). "Behold, how good and pleasant it is for brethren to dwell together in unity!" (Ps. 133:1 KJV)

I felt a strong sense of the anointing of God in our assembly at church on one certain Sunday morning. It occurred during our praises unto God. Jonathan is one of our very blessed, anointed, high praise leaders. One can observe his devout passion and desire to please God as he ministers in praise and worship. One of my favorite hymns, *The Hallelujah Anthem* (Todd Dulaney), was the song of praise. The congregation was engaging themselves to this wonderful moment. In a fleeting glance upward, toward the circular dome of the church, and I saw a thin cloud or mist. Beyond the mist, I saw a band of angels peering downward. They were divinely ordered to fill a perfectly circular alignment of space along the outer rim of the dome. Their garments were of an indescribably white brilliance, much like illuminating, fluorescent light. They were touching, wing-to-wing, with no space in between them, arrayed with God's glory. I wanted to capture this visitation as proof that they were there, but I could not look away for fear I would miss out on this momentous miracle. They vanished in unison but left a mark of conviction and belief in me like no other that I have experienced in the church—so awesomely divine! It was by far a visitation that was a bit beyond description: *angels inquiring in the house of God of things on earth that are not encountered in heaven?* Salvation through Jesus is for earthly beings, while heavenly things are already holy, just, and righteous!

> It was revealed to them that their services [their prophesies regarding grace] were not [meant] for themselves *and* their time, but for you, in these things [the death, resurrection, and glorification of Jesus Christ] which have now been told to you by those who preached the gospel to you by the [power of the] Holy Spirit [who was] sent from

heaven, into these things even the angels long to look. (1 Peter 1:12 AMP)

I thank our heavenly Father for the obedience of angels that we may know of His manifold glory as they are dispersed to bear good tidings, protection, and bring us comfort while we embrace the glory of Your presence. May we all be touched by Your presence and know that You are all that we need upon this earth, for life and godliness to the intent that "now unto the principalities (authority in celestial hierarchy) and powers in heavenly places might be known by the church, the manifold wisdom of God" (Eph. 3:10 NIV).

God's Homework: Your angel is watching over you right at this moment. We do not pray to them, but we can thank God for sending our guardian angels to watch over us. Whisper a prayer to God, thanking Him for angels and for His awesomeness in watching over you at this very moment.

20

Adventures of Unmerited Favor

SHELLEY M. FISHER, PH.D.

And so find favor and high esteem in the sight of God and man.
(Prov. 3:4 NKJV)

When I was in the educator's group, I became so hungry for the Word of God. I would attempt to satiate this hunger by attending conferences. It really did not matter that I had to go alone. I set out for Denver, Colorado, to see Marilyn Hickey. I had attended her conferences near my home, studying and hearing the Word for hours in her sessions called *Word Encounters*.

I craved another experience.

I had a friend there who I had not seen for years. She taught at the university in Denver. I intended to have lunch with her and catch up. I also envisioned riding the cable cars high into the mountains, perhaps in between sessions. My first trip to Denver was going to be memorable.

The conference was in downtown Denver at a major hotel. I only carried one bag. When I checked into the hotel my plan was to carry it myself to my room. After receiving my key, I turned to see a bellman grabbing my bag. Before I knew it, he had it in hand and was leading me to the elevator.

He asked, "Who are you?"

I answered, "Pardon me?"

He said, "I want to know who you are. Only famous people stay in your suite."

He went on to list a litany of actors and singers.

He asked again, "Who are you?"

I answered, "I'm a child of God."

He continued chattering about all the famous people who had occupied the suite.

We finally arrived at a palatial suite—three large rooms. I was in awe of my accommodations. I called my friend but got an answering service and requested that she return the call. On the way to the meetings downstairs, I quietly peeked into other rooms if I passed a door that was open. They all looked like my version of familiar hotel rooms.

At registration I received my name tag. People were there from all over the world. As I was alone, I was anxious to meet new friends. The first group of ladies I met were from Asia but now lived in the United States. Since we were all intercessors, I told them of my spacious suite and invited them up to pray in between sessions.

As I met more and more attendees, they would join us for prayer in between sessions. We used the suite to petition God for our nation and our fellow man. God gave me a beautiful room. He favored me with these lavish accommodations. This was my way of giving it back to Him, as we interceded during the conference.

The general session meetings were anointed. Both the Word and gifts from Marilyn Hickey flowed. I never heard from my friend but did get to ride the cable cars into the mountains with some of my fellow intercessors. Most of all, the Word broke forth in intercessory prayer from a group of ladies who had a distinctly international flavor.

Another time I experienced extraordinary favor was on a trip with my family to South Africa. At the onset of our trip, the tourists introduced themselves to each other. The historical church where our guide had planned for us to worship had closed. She lamented on our sight-seeing tour that we would not be able to gather there. Later in the day, after the daily tour, our guide asked me if I would preach to the group the following day. Out of one hundred people, she remembered my introducing myself as an educator and minister. I was elated and agreed to conduct the Sunday service.

The next morning, after breakfast, the group assembled in a meeting room in the hotel. I preached the Lord Jesus. It is always a pleasure and honor to preach the Word, but I was especially thrilled that I was given the opportunity to preach on the continent of Africa. I believe God ordained my experience in Africa before the foundation of the world—before there was a when or a where. The Word says, "For I know the plans I have for you, declares the Lord, "plans to prosper you and not to harm you, plans to give you hope and a future" (Jer. 29:11 NIV). Hallelujah!

God's Homework: In the Scripture: "Let the favor of the Lord our God be upon us and establish the work of our hands upon us; yes, establish the work of our hands!" (Ps. 90:17 KJV). *Favor* implies beauty, kindness, and grace from God. Think of the times God gave you favor and praise Him.

21

Glossolalia: Speaking in Tongues

SHELLEY M. FISHER, PH.D.

Likewise the Spirit also helpeth our infirmities for we know not what we should pray for as we ought: but the Spirit itself maketh intercession for us with groanings which cannot be uttered. (Rom. 8:26 KJV)

Glossolalia—speaking in tongues—has long been controversial in the church community. My denomination does not advocate glossolalia. It was while the teachers were housed at the high school, during the custodial strike, when they decided to have church meetings with Bible study, prayer, and preaching that I heard some of them speaking in tongues. Before then, I knew nothing about it.

That evening at church the Girl Scout leaders assembled and the topic of teachers speaking in tongues was foremost on their minds. I did not have a heightened reaction because I knew so little about it. But I was not frightened by their actions like others seemed to be. Some in our group of scout leaders were appalled that educators would participate in such an activity. Others said that the act of speaking in tongues vanished 2000 years ago. We finally got on with our scout meetings after much ado.

I did not realize that God had a plan to strengthen me and to take me to the next level. I continued attending the meetings at Gary Educators for Christ. I even joined my mentor's spiritual group in Chicago. I was thirsty and hungry for the more of God. I learned to quiet my thoughts and listen to God's voice. In the way that God speaks to me, I felt impelled to ask Him about speaking in tongues. I went to my then denominational pastor and asked him about glossolalia. He sent my husband home from church with a stack of books on the topic.

I devoured each of them voraciously, but I would not get far into the pages of a particular book before something inside me signaled it was the wrong information. This continued to happen to me as I read one book after another. The books basically said the act of speaking in tongues disappeared 2000 years ago. The message was essentially that if it occurred in our present day, it was not an act of God. My reading was short-lived. I returned the books and thanked my pastor.

I kept seeking God about my desire to pray in the spirit with the evidence of speaking in tongues. I continued reading the Word and listening to the voice of God. A co-worker and a member of the educator's group would ask me intermittently if I were ready to speak in tongues.

My reply was, "Not yet. I'm working on it."

Finally, one day she came by my classroom and asked the question once again.

I replied with certainty, "I am ready to receive."

After I took my children home from school and settled them in, I went to her home. She prayed for me to receive the baptism of the Holy Spirit, which is also called speaking in tongues or glossolalia. Right away, I lifted my arms and began to speak in tongues. I felt my arms waving from side to side and this beautiful language flowed from the pit of my stomach. I felt peace overtake me. I have been speaking in tongues ever since.

The change that came to me was a love for God and a commitment to do His will. A new boldness had come over me. I prayed more, studied my Bible more, and learned to hear God's voice. My mentor, the leader of the educator's group, prophesied to me about speaking the Word all over my city. She said I had a prophetic ministry gift. There was increase after increase in various areas of my life.

No one told me about "travailing." Roman 8:26 (KJV), says that when we know not how to pray as we ought, the Spirit makes utterances for us with groanings that cannot be understood. One evening at home, when my husband had taken our two children to after-school activities, I started praying in tongues. I began to groan and moan. My inner being felt wretched. My thoughts ran the gamut: *You do not know what you're doing. What have you gotten yourself into? You are always exploring stuff.* But my experience can be found in Romans 8:26. When I did not know how to pray, the Spirit prayed His perfect will through groaning and moaning.

My repertoire of praying has expanded. Now I know how to pray as Paul said, "Well then, what shall I do? I will pray in the spirit, and I will also pray in words I understand. I will sing in the spirit, and I will also sing in words I understand" (1 Cor. 14:15 NLT). Allow the Holy Spirit to teach you about speaking in tongues.

God's Homework: How open are you about things that are non-traditional in your denomination? When we do not know how to pray as we ought, the Spirit makes intercessions for us with groanings which cannot be understood. In your Bible study, read about speaking in tongues. Can you discern any advantages? In the Book of Acts note the difference in Peter's behavior after the day of Pentecost. Ask the Holy Spirit to teach you about this phenomenon.

22

A Glimpse into Another Realm with The Lens of the Supernatural

✿

ERNESTINE MEADOWS MAY

For the weapons of our warfare are not carnal but mighty through God to the pulling down of strongholds. (2 Cor. 10:4 KJV)

I have been given a gift to experience a realm that the natural senses cannot operate within. There is the dark side of the supernatural, as well as the glory that can dispel all darkness. Many people do not want to go there—and I am one of those people—but God has put in me a position to do so. I have been given a level of trust that brings me to the place of facing what is real in the earth and to remain aware of the necessity of the pulling down of strongholds. God wants us to be on guard and aware at all times. We cannot afford to be fearful of the unknown. Fear begins in the mind, with wrong thinking and with not knowing the authority of the Word and power of God endowed upon us by the Holy Ghost. Satanic presentations are intimidating and can be overwhelming when we're focusing on the content of our senses and emotions. Think of yourself as having a "sixth sense of the spirit." And know this as well: Satan has followers, but he is not loyal to any, for his purpose is to steal, kill, and destroy. He uses his hold over others to manipulate them as pawns to fulfill his will. But God—remember the facts stated in Luke 10, He (Jesus) has given us "power to tread on serpents and scorpions, and *over all the power of the enemy*: and nothing shall by any means hurt you" (Luke 10:19 emphasis added KJB). As in First John 1, we must declare "Greater is He that is in us than he that is in the world" (1 John 1:4 KJV).

After I had been through a myriad of dreams, visitations, and visions, I became acquainted with the ways of the enemy. He was attempting to put fear in me, intimidate me, and break my faith in God, but in every external and internal experience, Jesus would show up. It was awesome! God allowed me to enter into enemy territories that I might know them for myself. He showed me how best to deal with Satan and all his imps. I didn't want to share those experiences with anyone because people are quick to judge.

"She's mad!" some might say.

Well yeah, I'm mad about Jesus! According to Ephesians 6, by faith, we can put on the garment of protection; the *helmet of salvation* (*to protect our minds),* our loins are girded about with truth (truth shall set us free), and wearing the *breastplate of righteousness* (no weapons); and our with feet shod with the preparation of the gospel of peace (walk in peace with all men); above all, taking *the shield of faith* (faith pleases God), wherewith we shall be able to quench all the fiery darts of the wicked. The battle calls for measures that are unfamiliar to the natural man. It is understood that this armor is necessary for opposing strongholds. When we know our God, we shall be strong and do great exploits in His name!

I still remain a bit surprised by the audacity of the devil coming into my dreams, while I must have seemed defenseless, to try and bully me! He must have believed he would have me at his will. I often could not speak during those times or move or even call out the name of the Lord to be my defense. I was completely restrained by Satan's attack on me. I did find that I could move my head from side to side and happily decided that I was not totally defenseless.

I began to repeat the Word of God in whispers in my mind, *"Greater is He that is in me that he that is in the world"* (1 John 4:4 KJV). Over and over, I repeated the verse until I felt a loosening of the hold over me. It could only be defined as a stronghold. I felt as though I had invisible shackles binding me. Those shackles began to fall off each time I repeated the Word of God in my spirit.

God spoke into my spirit saying, *"The Word* in you *works* for you!"*

That is why it is so important for us to know the Word of God. Being prepared by the Word is how we fight! Jesus used the Word when He allowed Himself to be taken up into the mountains to be tempted by Satan.

When you cannot pray, confess the Word found in 1 John 4: "Ye are of God little children, and have overcome them; because greater is he that is in me, then he that is in the world"(1 John 4:4 KJV). Or you can use Psalm 91: "A thousand may fall at your side, and ten thousand at your right hand; but it shall not come near me" (Ps. 91:7 NKJV). Or you can try Isaiah 54: "No weapon that is formed against you shall prosper and every lying tongue that shall come against you in judgment you will condemn" (Isa. 54:17). And be sure to remember Psalm 23: "Surely goodness and mercy shall follow you all the days of your life and you shall dwell in the House of the Lord forever" (Ps. 23:6 KJV). And finally, remind yourself continually of Isaiah 41: "Fear not, for I am with you; Be not dismayed, for I am your God. I will strengthen you, yes, I will help you, I will uphold you with my righteous right hand" (Isa. 41:10 NKJV). His promises are true. Activate the Word. It is a command of power centered on the Will of God, our Father.

I, along with others belonging to a group of faith-based believers, were invited by a principal at one of our schools to join her in prayer to release the power and anointing of God by faith, to destroy the works of the enemy prevailing in her jurisdiction. She was able to discern the signs.

We were asked to walk around the school building and pray. The enemy was already stirred up and would band forces to thwart our mission! I didn't realize the level of spiritual struggle it would reveal to me, but I soon found out. When we walked past the window of one of the teachers that had presented problems, I began to see images of a huddled mass of unclothed gray bodies intertwined and huddled one with the other. I could not see where one began or the next ended. They were growling and snarling because they had been disturbed. Just angry! It was difficult to know how many were there, but I was certain they could be characterized as legions. This took me aback as I viewed this through my spiritual lens. It was a confirmation of the root cause of projected evil in the building causing strife, division, envy, jealousy, and backbiting. The principal's concerns were justified. I believe I was on assignment to see into the spirit realm for myself. These evil spirits were comfortable where they were and very annoyed by our presence.

We had called them out through prayer and speaking the Word of God. Although we caused them to be aroused, they remained.

I later asked the Lord in prayer, *"Why didn't they leave when it was commanded of them to do so?"*

In my spirit I heard, *"They are the stubborn kind and have a deep refusal to obey."* My takeaway was that we needed to arm ourselves with more weaponry. We needed to be even more aggressive and confident in what we were speaking, storing more Word inside ourselves as ammunition, and increasing our fasting and prayer. We were not done!

We're not always going to be one hundred percent, but we can continue to grow in grace and from glory to glory by each experience in life. It was quite the lesson to learn and to see firsthand that the enemy is also a bully who lies, perverts the truth, steals our goods, kills, and destroys. Nevertheless, in the Name of Jesus, he is a defeated foe! We are victorious and forever standing to hold up the banner for our Lord! In the end, Jesus is our overcomer! We have been redeemed by the blood of the Lord. Isaiah 14 says it this way: "They that see him (the devil) shall narrowly look upon him and consider . . . saying, ``Is this the man that made the earth to tremble, that did shake kingdoms?" (Isa. 14:16 KJV). My prayer is that the Almighty God, our Savior, would open our eyes of understanding to the knowledge of His power—in Jesus' Name. Learn from Him and see the reward of your effort.

God's Homework: Take a short walk around the perimeter of your home, inside and out, and as you walk, repeat this Scripture: (personalize it as follows) "I AM brave and courageous—for the Lord, MY God is with ME wherever I may go" (Ephesians 10:4).

23

Dreams, Visions, and Visitations in Japan

⌇

SHELLEY M. FISHER, PH.D.

For even though I am absent in body I am nevertheless
with you in spirit, rejoicing to see your orderly manner and
the stability of your faith in Christ. (Col. 2:5 NASB)

Ezekiel says, "I sought for a man among them, that should make up the hedge, and stand in the gap before me for the land, that I should not destroy it; but I found none" (Ezek. 22:30 NIV). Of all ministries, I consider intercessory prayer my priority. When we pray for others, God takes care of our business. Even more importantly, He promises that "He will deliver one who is not innocent, who will be delivered through the cleanness of your hands." (Job 22:30 NIV).

My basement was my place of prayer. It was where I did my walking and talking to God about issues. One day, the Lord showed me a vision which seemed to take place in an abandoned warehouse. It was dreary and dimly lit. I was not familiar with the location. People were gathered there. The leader of the group seemed to be preaching as the crowd listened attentively. Everyone was Asian. I watched as the speaker praised the name of Jesus. Afterwards, the people began to pray in one voice. I watched and listened, wondering if this was something to come?

Never having spoken a word aloud, the Lord brought my attention to a display of Japan that I currently had on my school bulletin board. I realized these people were Japanese and were worshiping Jesus in secret. I knew they could be punished for doing so. They read in Japanese from their Bibles. They were excited about Jesus. They smiled and chatted, responded to the leader, and would even pray in tongues at various times.

The Lord showed me this was a clandestine meeting. I had no other way of envisioning these activities. My assignment was to pray for their protection, so they would not be detected. I saw their faces clearly and witnessed their love for God, even though I did not understand their language. For three months I interceded for this group. I prayed until the Lord released me.

God's ways are not our ways. He is not limited by time or space. He will accomplish His will on the earth. We should never try to limit God to the boundaries of our capacity. He is omniscient, omnipotent, and omnipresent. Our limitations are not His limitations. He needed an intercessor to pray for the group in the warehouse and I was available, willing, and obedient.

The Bible is replete with stories of people having visions. One that has always impressed me was when Peter was hungry, waiting for dinner to be prepared, and he went up on the rooftop. There he saw a sheet come down that was filled with animals which he considered unclean to eat.

The Lord spoke, "Peter, rise, slay, and eat."

Peter answered, "No, my Lord. I will never eat anything unclean."

The Lord responded, "What I have cleansed do not consider unclean" (Acts 10:13–15).

This vision is a representation of the Lord bringing the gentiles into His kingdom. In a different part of the same vision, Peter saw some men coming to his house. The Lord instructed him to go with them. The visions became a reality when Peter went to Cornelius's house. Cornelius was a gentile, Roman soldier who prayed to God earnestly, paid alms, but still was not saved. Peter led Cornelius and his household to salvation. This was the first gentile family to receive salvation (Acts 10:44).

God is seeking those who are willing and obedient to do His will. He promises that if you are willing and obedient you will eat the good of the land (paraphrased Isaiah 1:19). Dreams and visions are ways that the Father speaks. Can He use you outside of your realm of understanding?

There are no boundaries in the spirit. God can use a person on one continent to interact with or to intercede on behalf of someone on another continent.

God's Homework: There is no distance in the Spirit. Do you know your assignment? God wants to take you places in the Spirit where you have never been to get His work done on the earth. He reaches you through the Spirit, intercession, and His work. There are no boundaries in Him. Purpose to sit quietly to hear God's voice. Record what he tells you and shows you; then obey.

24

What Do You Think of Me?

⚶

SHELLEY M. FISHER, PH.D.

And because of him you are in Christ Jesus who became to us wisdom from God, righteousness and sanctification and redemption. (1 Cor. 1:30 ESV)

I had a dream about a conference with hundreds of women in attendance. We were walking around, laughing and fellowshipping together. The sessions had ended, and the evaluations were ready. I was not sure if I had been a presenter or an attendee. I also do not know the role of the person I was trying to ingratiate myself to, but she had to do with the evaluations. She called me over and handed me a card. I opened the card to see an evaluation score of .011. My brain was working hard to translate what my eyes were seeing. I thought, *Oh, my goodness, I am not worth a whole number.* Then, I began to laugh hilariously in the dream, so much so that I woke myself up.

Evaluations were an integral part of my duties as a principal. A rating registering below a whole number was unthinkable. When I researched the spiritual significance of my score in the dream, I discovered it meant "new beginnings" and that "new doors will open." The lesson from the dream was clear to me. It does not matter what people think about you. God's plan is what counts.

There is a body of Scripture that defines who we are in Christ Jesus and what we have in Him. The verses explain our real and authentic identities. The Word says we are the righteousness of God, each of us is a joint heir with Jesus, and more than a conqueror (Rom. 8:16–17, 37; 1 John 5:11–12 KJV). As we study our Bibles, we can take note of all the Scriptures that can break our patterns of feeling inferior or helpless. When we know we are in right standing with God, a joint heir with Him, and more than a conqueror, how can our thoughts not be elevated?

"For in Him we live and move and have our being" (Acts 17:28 KJV). This verse denotes an intimate connection to God. Our very being—mind, will, and emotions—are immersed in Him. His attributes become who we are. How can we fear making wrong decisions or what others can do to us? When we are ensconced in Him, the two become one. The spiritual journey becomes eventful, powerful, and exciting.

First Corinthians 5 speaks to one's newness in Christ: "Wherefore if any man is in Christ Jesus, He is a new creature. Old things have passed away. All things have become new" (1 Cor. 5:17 KJV). It does not matter what we have done, where we come from, or who we may think we are or are not, Jesus wipes our slates clean and welcomes us to a new life in Him. We can come to understand we have become new creatures in Him, allowing us so many possibilities. Our past is gone, and new beginnings are ahead of us.

"Romans Road" represents the onset of the new life. "If you believe in your heart and "confess with thy mouth the Lord Jesus . . . thou shalt be saved. For with the heart man believeth unto righteousness; and with the mouth confession is made unto salvation" (Rom. 10:9–10 KJV). There are miracles in our mouths. This hearty confession before God, along with Christ's resurrection, brings us into relationship with Jesus, with new horizons and depths to be realized.

One final Scripture to round off this newness is: "Christ in you the hope of glory" (Col. 1:27 KJV). We are supernatural; just as Christ is, so are we. The hope of glory is in us—power, ability, fire to do the work of the ministry and be overcomers of obstacles to move in victory. We do not need man's approval, for God has already ordained us and has a plan for our lives.

God's Homework: You are valuable to God. Do not let people define who you are. If they have a problem with you, your gifts, and abilities, that is their problem to handle. Know who you are and that you are important in the kingdom of God. Study the Scriptures that tell you who you are and what you have in Christ Jesus.

25

To Russia with Love

GLORIA SHARPE SMITH

Also I heard the voice of the Lord, saying, Whom
shall I send, and who will go for us? Then said
I, Here am I; send me. (Isa. 6:8 KJV)

Living out the Scripture above became a reality for me in September 2004. I was very involved in missions. The majority of my activities were taking place locally and through giving to a select group of mission organizations. The thought of doing an international mission trip did not occur to me until one Sunday while I was attending an afternoon worship service. The guest speaker told us about a trip that she was preparing to embark upon, and I listened with admiration to her commitment. She asked for donations to purchase shoes for the children in the village that she would be visiting. I contributed with delight.

A few weeks later, I was visiting with a friend. She mentioned that Marie, a missionary we both knew, was planning a trip to Russia and was looking for others to travel with her. Immediately, in my spirit I heard, "*GO.*" A peace and excitement stirred in my soul. I knew that God had spoken to me. I told my friend to give Marie a call and tell her that I was interested in going. The next most important thing for me to consider was how to tell Ernest, my husband. I prayed and asked God to prepare his heart. The decision about my going would be left up to him.

My husband asked only one question, "How do you know God wants you to go to Russia?"

I explained to him about the series of events that led to my decision.

He said, "Do what God told you to do."

I had his blessings and permission. Neither my peace, nor passion, ever wavered concerning any aspect of the trip. There were weeks of praying, planning, and collecting items to carry and distribute.

I asked the Lord, "What should I tell the people?"

He said, *"Tell them that I have called you to go, love, and serve."*

The Great Commission is about loving, sharing, giving, and caring. This is what the Lord intends for Christians to do. God was giving me an opportunity to share love and be a blessing to orphans, prisoners, and some of the most forgotten people of Saransk, Russia. God opened a door for us to utilize our gifts and talents in service to teach, preach, sing, and distribute Bibles.

We worked with a Russian General who was also a Christian.

He told us, "Saransk is a place that none of the missionaries want to come to because the conditions are so poor. It is very difficult to get any aid for these people and the orphans are the most severely disabled. They are the children that no one wants."

I believe God felt differently. My friend had taken over twenty-one trips to Russia at that time. She had an ongoing relationship with several hospitals, orphanages, and local churches. Both her passion and ministry were aimed at providing supplies, monetary gifts, encouragement, and Bibles. I felt blessed that God was allowing me to serve with her.

One day, as I was going through my closet looking for items to donate, I became fixated on a beautiful, two-piece ensemble that was practically brand new. It was a size eight. I remember thinking, *"This probably won't fit anyone over there."* My image of Russian women didn't fit my dress size. The skirt and long sleeve blouse were a beautiful shade of grey, complimented by pale pink, lemon yellow, and light orange flowers with green leaves. The fabric was soft and flowed gracefully when worn. "*Take it!*" an inner voice said. I took both pieces from the closet and placed them in the pile with the other items that were going to Russia with love.

We further prepared to be a blessing by assembling various gift bags containing hotel-sized shampoos, lotion, soap, toothpaste, deodorant, packets of tissue, photo albums, small jewelry items, mittens, scarves, coloring books, hair ribbons, and cosmetic bags.

We also collected baseball caps because we were told that Russians loved them. Logos didn't matter as long as there wasn't any mention of bodily functions, sexual innuendos or any writing that advertised alcohol or cigarettes. People were very generous in their giving. I was overjoyed with the positive responses from everyone I'd contacted regarding donations.

When the deadline for donations rolled around, we had enough items to fill sixteen large pieces of stowaway luggage, but we were only allowed two personal pieces each on our tickets. There were three of us traveling together. That meant six pieces would be free and ten would have to be paid for. We were told that each additional piece of luggage would cost $120. My church family and other generous donors covered the cost. God was faithful in meeting that need; however, as it turned out, we didn't have to pay for the extra luggage. When we arrived at O'Hare International Airport to check in, the ticket agent was very curious about the amount of luggage that we had. Marie, our friend and mission coordinator, explained the purpose for the trip and the contents of the luggage. She also presented a letter from the director of the missions organization requesting that the fees be waived, and they were! This generous waiver provided us with additional funds to give to various churches, orphanages, and schools. We gave away everything. I was in awe of the gesture and considered it a miracle from God to help those in need. I felt that He was showing me His heart and concern for people I didn't know—but He did.

When we arrived at the airport in Moscow, it was late in the day and our host/interpreter was not there to meet us. I was with Marie, and she assured me that everything would be fine. Finally, our luggage came off the conveyor belt and we gathered all sixteen pieces. This is when a test of our faith kicked in. We had to pass through customs and explain all of our luggage. It had to be visually inspected; it was going to take some time. None of the luggage was locked, so gaining access was easy. We were escorted to a side of the airport's exit door and could see people leaving and greeting those who were waiting for them. After the customs agent had inspected about five of the pieces, he opened one that was completely filled with diabetic supplies. He had been logging in the contents of every piece. He became frustrated in his attempt to count and log the items.

"Go, go," he said.

It was my first indication that he understood one word of English.

All during this time, the three of us had been standing to the side watching, praying, and singing to the glory of God. Our prayers had been answered and, just like that, we were free to go and take all of our luggage. And wouldn't you know, just as we got clearance, the host walked up!

"Thank you, Jesus," was my greeting to him.

It was now very late in the evening. There was no time to tour Moscow. We had been held captive in customs for six hours. We went directly to our hotel and retired for the night. The next day, our host arrived right on time. We began the eight-hour ride to Saransk. My mind constantly wondered about what was to come. I was so far away from everything and everyone that I knew, yet I knew within my heart that I was exactly where I was supposed to be. I had perfect peace and so did the other two women with me.

Words cannot express the joy that I felt when we finally arrived at the church where our host pastor, his petite wife, and several other members of his small, warm, and welcoming congregation greeted us. No words were shared, just smiles and the loving spirit that connected us. It felt as though we were known to one another. It was divine. All of the luggage was unloaded at the church, where it would stay until we removed portions daily to distribute at the various places where we ministered.

We had breakfast daily at the church. The pastor's wife was always available to serve us joyfully. She and the other women took delight in watching us eat and say our grace before the meal. There was such peace and purpose associated with everything on my agenda each day that I never had time to long for home. During the time that I was in Saransk, I learned that the heating system for all of the community was controlled by the Russian government. It was late September, and the heat would not be turned on until the first part of October. It was cold, but we were too early to get heat. What to do? Pray! And that's what I did. I prayed for God to make an exception for us and turn the heat on early. He answered that prayer and also rewarded me for my obedience and faith.

Before I left home, my spiritual mother invited me to her home for lunch. She gave me a generous donation and a heavy, large, bulky, red and white bathrobe. She told me to take it to Russia. I was a little concerned about that because of the luggage restrictions and the amount of space that the bulky robe would require. Nonetheless, I packed it and later thanked God that I did. It was the blanket that I desperately needed and appreciated on those cold nights when there was no heat. God provides. He regards obedience. I still have the robe and delight in putting it on when needed, but also when I want to reflect on something that makes me feel special.

Ministering in and around Saransk was a time of serving that I'll cherish forever. There were many special and rewarding moments for me. But the one that made my heart dance occurred on the Sunday morning before returning home. As I stated earlier, we would have breakfast at the church daily and the pastor's wife would always greet us. I always looked forward to seeing her and enjoying the meal. It was a little different on this Sunday morning. She didn't greet us. I wondered where she was but didn't inquire. After I had greeted the other church members, I was preparing to join the praise circle. One of the ladies came running towards me and motioning with her hands for me to come. She was leading me in a direction that I wasn't familiar with—to the kitchen. After a few briskly paced steps, my eyes widened, and my jaw dropped! My spirit began to soar with joy and amazement. There she stood with arms wide open and a smile that lit up the room. Other people were standing around her and pointing as if to say, "Look." The pastor's wife was wearing the grey, floral, size 8, two-piece ensemble. She looked beautiful, dancing joyously around in a circle that seemed to praise God! I'm sure that she was feeling the love and joy that only God could provide. She had chosen that outfit as the one item that only she could wear. I didn't encounter another woman who could have worn it. It had traveled all the way from America just for her.

The interpreter told me that when the pastor's wife first saw the outfit she'd said, "It's the most beautiful dress that I've ever seen and it's from God for me!"

God knows how to make our joy full and delight us with pleasures beyond our imagination.

My mission to Russia was filled with love and blessings, both as a giver and receiver. The robe warmed me, while the outfit blessed the pastor's wife. I traveled back home with a new appreciation for how God provides and with a renewed realization of the care that He takes in meeting our needs. Missionary work, when done as service to the Lord, is beyond rewarding and I invite you to go when you're called. You may never be called to travel to Russia or any other foreign place; however, you will be called to help meet the need of someone, somewhere, someday. Will you GO?

God's Homework: Obey the voice of God today, without hesitation concerning whatever He instructs you to do.

26

A Vision of Piccadilly in London

❦

ERNESTINE MEADOWS MAY

*Now the law came in to increase trespass, but where sin
increased, grace abounded all the more.* (Rom. 5:20 ESV)

There is a possibility that your waking moments can best be
managed and controlled by you, but the second you close your
eyes and drift off to another dimension, you cannot control the
invasions of your psyche or spirit. In this way we become the ben-
eficiaries of more than we can explain or even interpret. Dreams
can be just that—a dream. I am a dreamer! I can remember some
of them, but most become lost, never to be realized ever again. In
my younger days I was asked if I dreamed in black-and-white or
if my dreams were in color. I had never thought about it that way.
It was something for me to try to key in on when I dreamed. You
cannot tell yourself what to do in a dream. It just happens; however, I believe that you can condition your mind to go into a dream
with a thought that can materialize in some small way. I am by no
means a psychologist. I've experimented with a few little things
because I wanted to know why I entered a dream realm with both
unfamiliar people as well as familiar faces, and what's it all about.
I'm curious.

Dreaming is another whole life for me. Sometimes I feel as
though I live again in my other life. As I retire for bed at night, I

think about things that will take me into a place of experiencing pleasantries. I consciously decide that I will look for good things and slowly my dreams begin to change in the way I wanted to see them happen.

I am beginning to see visions with my eyes wide shut! My eyes are closed as I am drawn into ethers beyond the natural realm of things. I am given a warning in my body and the atmosphere around me changes to alert me that I will be entering another zone—and it's *not* the "Twilight" one! I don't get this warning if I dream, in other words, while I'm sleeping.

In this dream I was taken to a place where my inner being led me to believe that I was at Piccadilly Square in London. I later researched it and found a picture of a tri-cornered building near the corner of a street that looked like the one I saw in this open vision. Surrounding the building was a grayish ash that looked as though it could have been from a fallout. Perhaps it was the aftermath of a terrible explosion or maybe the devastation of a bombing attack. A dusty haze hung in the atmosphere and blanketed the entire city. Everything was an ashen gray.

During my dreams I think as I see, so I was also thinking the scene before my eyes could, perhaps, have taken place at the time of the rapture because certainly the Spirit of the Lord was absent in this place to the extent of what He will allow.

There were a few people in the streets, mostly men, walking in every direction. Not one of them met my glance. Grotesque looking men with their faces ranging from chalky white to gray, exhibited stark, blank stares through dark, almost hollow, eye sockets. These people moved about wordlessly. They passed me by as though I did not exist. And no wonder; I actually didn't because I was in the spirit, transported to another time and space. .Everyone appeared dirty and unclean. The common physique was quite slim. I was seeing everything at once. I was readying to cross the street when I saw this bobbie (members of London's Metropolitan Police are called bobbies, which is derived from the name of Sir Robert Peel, who established the force in 1829, https://www.britannica.com>topic) who also looked unreal. His tall, black dome-like hat and the tri-cornered building at the intersection helped me to identify with where I was. Some people were riding bikes, others were walking, but I also noticed a car that caught my attention. It was a small vehicle, similar to the Smart Hybrid model, with seating for only two people. I don't know where I was trying to get to. I wanted to identify with something, so I could stay in touch with my sanity. After I crossed the street, there was a stack of mannequins at the back corner of the building near the alley. They looked like dead, stiff people. At first, I thought they were actual humans—very weird looking!

A truck approached and slowly passed me. I could see a man with one half of his face painted a chalky white and the other half revealed facial disfigurements, as well as more on his body. He had two passengers in his truck. One of them had a long wig hanging on the left side of his head.

A loudspeaker attached to the truck was blaring full blast, "Seeking two young boys to ride with us."

I was thinking, "*Am I hearing correctly?*" I knew what they wanted. The spirit of lasciviousness came to mind. Revelation knowledge permeated my sixth sense, letting me know that the spirit in them was the cause of their crippled bodies and minds. This action seemed oblivious to me because it was so commonplace.

I kept thinking it was imperative to get to the place that was propelling me to the unknown. It seemed to be my mission to show up there, perhaps a stadium or the like. All I know is that I was drawn to go there. I came out of the vision, not knowing where I was or why I was in this place. It could have been a place of refuge for me. The closest that I had come to speaking to someone, while having the vision, a young man on a bike was crossing the street. As he passed me, he seemed to say something about the directions as to where I was going. His speech was unclear, unintelligible and muffled.

This experience caused me to see inside another dimension to observe these considerations:

1. A world entertaining sexual abomination.
2. A glimpse of the earth after the rapture.
3. The look of sin through spiritual eyes.
4. A turn from God towards man's own pleasures.
5. What the earth is like without the presence of God's spirit.

A deeper thought to remember, which should be first and foremost, can be found in John 3: "For God so loved the world that He gave His only Son that whosoever believes in Him, shall not perish but shall have everlasting life"(John 3:16 KJV). This is the perfect gift to the world that is available to those who believe in Him, as the Scripture has said. To receive this free gift, it is imperative that we ask forgiveness of our sins, open up our hearts, and believe that God has sent Jesus—Who died once and for all as the ultimate sacrifice for us— to be our Savior. Ask Him to come into your heart, confess Him to be your Lord and Savior, and you shall be saved. Welcome to the family of God! We have been given a plan for life everlasting in Jesus. God will not give up on us, but He has set His judgment at the appointed time. Salvation is a gift of eternal life to every believer.

Following this vision, I went on to dream that I was walking through a place where a lady was praying behind a podium. It was a desperate, fervent, and a hard call out to God. It was a prayer that I had not heard before. I was looking to see if I knew her. But did not recognize her. The place was packed with people, but they were beginning to leave as she prayed. She addressed the issue of them leaving, but it seemed the people were hardhearted and did not want to have anything to do with this. Their leaving indicated their rejection of God. I stood, planted in my tracks. I looked around and recognized that I was inside the church. I had been a witness to the world's rejection of God. This dream was a conclusion supporting what I had seen in the vision. The theme being the rejection of God in the earth.

The experience was a reminder to me of the verse in John 4: "God is a spirit and they that worship Him must worship Him in spirit and in truth" (John 4:24 KJV). Let us continue to pray fervently and earnestly, declaring and decreeing the Word of God until it is established in the hearts of men and women. We must also remember Philippians 2: "When the Name of Jesus is spoken, every knee will bow to worship Him. Every knee in heaven and on earth and under the earth will bow and worship Him" (Phil. 2:10 NIV).

God's Homework: Go to your window, your opened door, or just look upward and simply say, "Father God, You are awesome in all of Your ways!"

27

Earthmoving Machinery

❧

Shelley M. Fisher, Ph.D.

*Sow righteousness for yourselves and reap in mercy, break up
your fallow ground: for it is time to seek the Lord, till he come
and rain righteousness upon you.* (Hosea. 10:12 KJV)

For years, I have had a vision of a giant steam shovel sitting
in the middle of several acres of hard ground. The soil is not
fallow but hard and dormant. There is nothing but hard, rocky soil
as far as the eye can see. The shovel extended downward into the
hardened dirt, but it was not making any indentation. This powerful machine could not break through the hard, dry surface.

I sense the Lord saying He is the shovel, calling man to repentance, to soften his hardened heart and return to Him. Just as the
priests of ancient times were corrupt, so are some of the pastors
and ministry gifts of today. There is too little interest in salvation.
There is too much emphasis on filthy lucre, money, for the advance-
ment of self. Instead of being the Lord's mouthpiece, voices have
gone silent, making them complicit with evil and wrongdoing on
the earth.

The Lord has strategically placed us on the seven mountains—Media, Government, Education, Economy, Religion,
Entertainment, and Family—and intends for man to conquer
these areas of influence and take the kingdom for Him.

The Lord has an indictment against us. We have turned from the Lord and hewn out cisterns and broken cisterns that can hold no water. *"Return to me,"* says the Lord. *"Break up your rocky ground, soften your hearts, and receive my love. Hear and obey. Repent and return to me. I await you with open arms."*

Ezekiel 36 says: "I will give you a new heart and put a new spirit within you. I will take away the stony heart out of your flesh, and I will give you a heart of flesh" (Ezek. 36:26 NKJV). God wants mankind to turn from the ways of the world and to focus on Him. When we worship Him in spirit and in truth, we will know there is work to be done in the kingdom, and we should commit to doing what is required of us.

God's Homework: How are you allowing God to use you to reach those whose hearts are hardened? What can you do? Praying for the lost and asking the Lord of the Harvest to send laborers into the field is something you can do. Praying for the lost to receive salvation is a way to help and impact the kingdom. You can also purposely set aside time to pray for the lost.

28

What...An Aroma in Christ?

⌒⚹⌒

SHELLEY M. FISHER, PH.D.

For we are to God the sweet aroma of Christ...
(2 Cor. 2:15 Berean)

Would you think it absurd if someone told you that Christ has an aroma? Well, I'm positive that you cannot convince me or twenty-four particular fifth grade students otherwise regarding the sweet smell of Jesus. On a sunny afternoon after lunch, my students noticed that I had changed clothing. They wanted to know why. I told them that I would be speaking to a group after school.

For the next five minutes, they contributed advice.

"If you get nervous, just look above the heads of your audience."

"You can do it Mrs. Fisher—pretend that the audience does not have clothes on and laugh so you won't get nervous."

I told them I would take their advice into consideration. It felt so good to hear their support. Then, something happened that we could not explain. The air was suddenly filled with a sweet fragrance. I asked who brought their mom's perfume to school.

"Give it up. Bring it to me now."

They looked puzzled. One by one, they responded by denying the possession of any perfume. Yet, the fragrance was sweet and mild. The children began to comment on the aroma as well.

"Wow, what is it? I like the smell."

The sweet-smelling odor continued to waft through the room for most of the afternoon. I believe we had a visitation—the sweet smell of Jesus.

The Bible has much to say about the sweet aroma of Jesus. Second Corinthians 2 tells us: "For we are to God the sweet aroma of Christ among those who are being saved and those who are perishing, to one a fragrance from death to death, to the other a fragrance from life to life. Who is sufficient for these things?" (2 Cor. 2:15–16 ESV).

Other verses (paraphrased here) let us know the gospel of Jesus Christ brings a sweet fragrance to those who are being saved; it has the aroma of victory. God uses us to spread the sweet fragrance of the knowledge of Him in every place. Christ-filled lives are like a lovely perfume (2 Cor. 2:14–17; 4:7–12).

In Ephesians 5:3 (KJV), Paul admonishes us to walk in love: "Therefore be imitators of God as dear children. And walk in love, as Christ also has loved us, an offering and a sacrifice to God for a sweet-smelling aroma." just as Christ also loved you and gave Himself up for us, an offering, and a sacrifice to God as a fragrant aroma."

And finally, God, speaking to His people: "As a soothing aroma, I will accept you when I bring you out from the peoples and gather you from the lands where you are scattered; and I will prove Myself holy among you in the sight of the nations" (Ezekiel 20:41 NASB).

God expresses love for His people in a myriad of ways. He is not confined by time, place, or audience. God's voice in the Scriptures is characterized as a soothing aroma. What an honor to have experienced this manifestation of God.

God's Homework: God calls you a sweet aroma of Christ among those who are being saved and from those who are perishing. Christ has loved us and has given Himself for us as an offering and sacrifice of God for a sweet-smelling savor (Exodus 29:18 NKJV).

When we give God our worship and praise, it is a sweet-smelling savor to Him. He longs for our praise and worship.

29

Heaven's Music in My Ears

ᑳᐟᕀᑐ

ERNESTINE MEADOWS MAY

It shall come to pass that before they call, I will answer, and while they are still speaking, I will hear. (Isa. 65:24 KJV)

This was by far one of the most intense visions that I have experienced. It began in the very wee hours of the morning and would transform how I would see through my spiritual being and believe the voice of God. The vision was set up for me. God wanted me to know the deep awesomeness of His being. His supernatural ways defy all laws of science and the natural state of the universe. In nature, we have boundaries where the laws of physics state that certain things are impossible. But through the supernatural, we can see possibilities that go directly against any reasonings and logical explanations we may have learned.

Earlier, I had been thinking about how awesome it would be to steal away for a period of time just to be with the Lord. I yearned for a secluded place without the interruptions of life's happenings—no other voice, no other visuals, and no other focus. I genuinely wanted to have this experience with my Creator, but I had a family at home and that took all of my attention—when I wasn't working. I would have considered it a personal retreat to bond with the Holy Spirit. He gives us the desire of our heart, but do not expect the expected! His thoughts are far beyond what we can ask or think because He is the all-wise, all-knowing God who is everywhere we are—He is our Abba.

Turns out, I didn't need to go off anywhere and disrupt family time to be with Him. God is so mindful of us. He knows our situation and will meet us where we are. As He says in Luke 12: "*Fear not little flock, it is your Father's good pleasure to give you the kingdom*" (Luke 12:32 KJV). The headboard on my bed, at the time, had a place for storage. It would be considered by some to be a convenience for a clock radio or even a few books. I never slept with the television or radio on. In fact, I rarely listened to the radio at that time. My radio was so old I don't know why I kept it around. I reckon it was because it still worked. It's hard to get rid of something that is still in good working order. Little did I know that my old radio would play such a crucial part in my experience.

I am a pretty sound and deep sleeper. In the wee hours of one morning, I began to hear a sound like I have never heard in all my life. I eventually recognized that it was coming from the radio and thought, "*But who turned it on?*" The dial of the radio was scanning through all of the stations on the dial. It sounded the same as if one were dialing to get to a specific station you're looking for. My instinct was to open my eyes, but I wasn't sure if what was happening would cease. I sensed the supernatural and was thinking, "*Welcome, Holy Spirit . . . come.*" The radio dial settled on music that was nothing short of heavenly. I could hear the words of heavenly angelic voices singing along with the music. I wanted to grab a pencil and paper to record the beautiful lyrics. The words were in praise of God, our Father. I knew that it was not a time to interrupt. I decided I would memorize the words, so that I could tell them to others. I lifted my head from the pillow slowly, and when I did, the music ceased. I didn't want it to stop before it was time, so I gently laid my head back down on the pillow and the music resumed. I was fully conscious of what was happening only my eyes remained closed. This music had never been played on earth's soil. It was indescribable and could not be duplicated—a beauty that could not be released at this time. It was glorious! I believed it was designed, orchestrated, and presented as a glimpse of the revelation of His glory. I am thankful that He revealed it to me. This memory is everlasting. I was learning how to follow the instructions issued in Psalm 46: *"Be still and know that I am God"* (Ps. 46:10 NIV).

My trust is in the Lord. I felt hands lifting and crossing my arms over my chest, then at my ankles, crossing them as well. Although I did not see it, I sensed a fine, dry, misty blanket in my room. With this anointing came a consuming peace, joy, and comfort, along with a lightness that I never knew before. There was a loving *presence* in the room.

My entire body began to gently float upwards towards the ceiling. As I drifted, I glanced down at my bed and saw myself lying there. I reached the ceiling and floated right through it and continued drifting onward through the entire roof of my house, sailing above houses and over the power lines, right through brick walls, and under fences. At first, I anticipated obstacles, but there were none. They did not exist because I trusted the vision. There was this sense of, *"Fear not."* I was interacting in the vision God had given to me. In my spirit, and as I wondered about the experience, I heard a reassurance that I would go through some things in life; that some of them I would rise above. There would be valley experiences and each encounter would bring me to an expected end. I had only to trust! I remembered Psalm 4: *"In peace will I lie down and sleep, for you alone, Lord, make me dwell in safety"* (Ps. 4:8 NIV).

When my physical body and my spirit met back up, I felt all my nerve endings tingling. My head began to throb. The physical me was impacted by this awesome power of the Spirit returning me to my abode!

The glory of the Lord had filled the room and now that His Presence had receded from the place where I beheld Him, I heard a very convincing voice say to me, *"Call Doretha!"* It was still early, but I wanted to give her time to rise. My mouth was pulsating. Normally, we would call each other concerning prayer, but at this juncture it was, *"Call for Doretha to come and lay her hands on me!"* I needed a touch. God had already anointed her for the service.

I made the call for her to come, but evidently God didn't tell her. She was on the phone to someone else. I didn't want to overly excite her, so I told her to call me back as soon as she finished her call. It seemed minutes had lapsed, then hours. I was wondering if she would remember to call me back. I was screaming inside, *"Doretha, I need you now!"* She called back and I asked if she could come over and she agreed. I wasn't going to be any good to anyone in the state that I was in. It was a Saturday, so no worries about work or early risers.

When Doretha arrived, it had only been about ten minutes since I had last spoken with her. She didn't know my needs and I didn't explain. She only knew I needed prayer. She began to pray. I took her hand and placed it on my head and immediately, *immediately,* I felt a diminishing of pain as it was released from every nerve in my body. I felt my entire body being refreshed and renewed, as though it contained the glory it was designed to hold! This is hard to explain.

I began to wonder about the heavenly music that saturated me and without an audible answer, I received, from my spirit, that the music prepared me for the trip! David played the harp before Saul that caused the evil spirit to go away (1 Sam. 16:23). And "Music has the power to enchant the roughest people." This proverb comes from the play, *The Mourning Bride*, by William Congreve, an English playwright and poet of the late seventeenth and early eighteenth centuries.

Music has a way of piercing into the deepest parts of our soul. It assists in our expression of and our responses to God. The infusion of music into this vision relaxed my body and changed the tempo of the ethers around me. I was nowhere, but somewhere. I thought not of tomorrow, nor did I remember yesterday. I became immersed in the response of heavenly doings. There was no part for me to play. I succumbed and totally surrendered to His presence.

Over time, I've come to understand much of the spiritual journey, visitations, and visions. I've asked God why the pain follows the trip. He let me know that the physical body cannot contain so great a power being released into it at any time. God wanted me to know the possibilities with Him.

We must wait on the Lord for deposits and understanding. He will reveal much to us in due season, if we trust Him. I was given a wonderful gift to share with others so that they may know that God is no respecter of person, according to Romans 2:11. What He does for one, He will do for others as well.

God's Homework: Offer up a seed prayer on behalf of those who come to your aid in times of distress:

"Father, I thank You for _____
I pray that You would bless him/her indeed this day, and I pray that his/her days will be long upon this earth. Amen."

Giving and Provision

30

Hidden from Natural Eyes

ERNESTINE MEADOWS MAY

For nothing is hidden that will not be made manifest, nor is anything secret that will not be known and come to light. (Luke 8:17 ESV)

I've always been a loser. A loser of things, that is! I'm thinking money, keys, documents, wallets, and other essential items. Some years ago, when the gaming boats opened their doors in our area, I went there to celebrate my birthday at one of the restaurants. It was something different and new. I was tempted to sit at one of the slot machines. My handbag laid on my lap while playing. In only a few moments, the bells and whistles of the machine alerted me that I had won a little windfall, which had me very excited. Although it was only two hundred dollars, it was my birthday. I considered it an unexpected gift. I jumped up with the ticket in hand that proved my bounty. I was looking for the nearest cash-out cage. I dashed over to the well-lit signage when I found it! I collected my two hundred dollars and realized I didn't have my handbag to keep it secure.

My heart sank at the realization that I had lost my purse with all of my money, credit cards, and my government identification. There must have been a hundred people to every square foot of space in that joint. *How would I be able to find my purse?* I had won, but lost, at the same time. *How was this possible?* I was just put out with myself! I rushed without running. I felt the blood pumping through my veins as my head was beginning to tighten, thinking of the long shot I had for finding my purse where I had been sitting. In all this, there was a calm inside the storm. It was the other me prompting my thoughts on *these* things. Similar happenings have occurred, and I came out the victor. If He did it once, He'll do it again. Put Him in remembrance of His Word. He is all-knowing, all-seeing, everywhere at the same time. Nothing is hidden from Him because He is the Alpha and Omega, Omnipotent, the Great *I AM*. My faith took me there! I silently prayed, *"Dear God, let all eyes be blind to the sight of my purse."*

This simple prayer was answered. Only my eyes saw where it had fallen to the floor between the stool where I'd been sitting and the machine I was playing. It seemed the area was darker there than I had remembered the time before. It was never lost in the sight of the Lord. He knew all along it was there and showed me His favor once again. Sometimes again, we just need to . . . *"Be still and know that He is God!"* (Ps. 46:10 NIV).

God's Homework: Make a list of things that you have lost or perhaps have had stolen from you. When you're finished, write out this statement of affirmation underneath:

"Lord,
I thank You that You will restore everything lost, taken, or stolen from me in a compounded way of return.
I thank You that it is so!
Amen."

31

Double the Pleasure

❧

GLORIA SHARPE SMITH

*Give, and it shall be given unto you; good measure, pressed
down, and shaken together, and running over, shall men give
into your bosom. For the same measure that you mete with
all it shall be measured to you again.* (Luke 6:38 KJV)

My refrigerator door used to be covered with souvenir magnets representing many of my travels, however, there was one in particular that didn't fit. It had an inscription that read, "Shop 'Til You Drop." It was a fun gift from a friend who shared my enthusiasm for shopping.

I cherished the act of browsing through the stores and buying gifts for other people. At our local mall, I always enjoyed stopping by the jewelry store to peer into the window at all of the exquisite pieces on display. One day, I saw a ring that I really liked and went into the store to inquire about it. The salesperson was quick to point out that the piece did not contain a diamond but was cubic zirconium. It was my first introduction to a stone that certainly looked like a real diamond to me. I wanted the ring. It was beautiful and affordable. I made my purchase and wore it daily for many years. The fact that it wasn't a real diamond didn't concern me—until I acquired a greater appreciation for fine jewelry. Sometime later, I decided I wanted some real diamonds. I had been perfectly content wearing my oversized, gold, wedding band with my cubic zirconium ring, but it was time for a change. Fast forward a year or so. I received a monetary Christmas gift from my oldest son, Vincent. My first thought was to use the money to purchase something special and lasting. I did my usual "quick thought prayer, "*Lord, my heart desires a real diamond ring. Please let me find something that I'll cherish.*"

During the Christmas season, my husband and I traveled to Los Angeles to be with Tony, our youngest son. During that time, of course, I went shopping. My mind was fixated on purchasing jewelry. I didn't have a clue as to what piece I wanted. I just knew that it would have to contain a real diamond. No more cubic zirconium for me. No more gold plated anything! I went into a jewelry store and spotted a beautiful white and yellow gold, diamond tennis bracelet that took my breath away. It was love at first sight. I asked the salesclerk if the stones were real diamonds.

He smiled and said, "Yes, they are. Would you like to try on this piece?"

"Yes, I would!"

I held my breath when I asked the price. When he told me, I said to myself, "*Thank You, Lord, this bracelet is mine.*"

I was a happy shopper, delighted in every way with my new jewelry. I considered the bracelet to be a gift from my son that would always be special. Back at home that evening, I told my husband and Sheree, our host, about my shopping experience and showed off my new bracelet.

My husband responded, "Very nice."

Sheree's response was far more enthusiastic. She admired my bracelet and said, "You like diamonds? I have some that I don't wear anymore. Let me show them to you."

I was amazed that I was speaking to a young woman who wasn't interested in wearing diamonds.

She went to her room, came back and said, "Look at these. Here are two rings that I purchased years ago when I first started working. I don't wear either of them anymore and you may have them."

I couldn't believe what I was hearing or seeing. Each ring was a different style and sparkled beautifully.

"What? You're kidding! Thank You!"

I was overwhelmed and amazed by her generosity. I had never experienced anyone giving me anything so freely and with such joy. She took delight in giving me something of value. She was a cheerful giver, and I was a grateful receiver. The exchange was complete. My experiences of that day taught me a valuable lesson. There are times when God will use us to bless others and there are times when He will use others to bless us. It's a real joy to participate in such a great and rewarding exchange. The giving and receiving of gifts can be both humbling and pleasurable. I think it's easier for us to give a gift than it is to accept one. We take delight in seeing someone's face light up when we give them things that they are pleased with. Yet, when we receive a gift, oftentimes, our response is, "Oh, you shouldn't have!" We have to learn how to receive graciously and simply say "Thank you." We must learn to acknowledge the pleasure in the exchange that takes place in being both the giver and the receiver.

God's Homework: Give something away to bring pleasure to someone else. Say "Thank you" without discounting the act of giving.

32

Found, but Not Lost

❧

SHELLEY M. FISHER, PH.D.

*Where can I go from Your Spirit? Or where can I
flee from Your presence?* (Ps. 139:7 NKJV)

I can remember wondering about the great God everyone talked about. I also remember joining a church congregation at age nineteen, because I was going away to college. At that point, I had learned that God would take care of me. I did not know what my future held, and I wanted His protection. My religious background did not include any teachings on spiritual gifts, the laying on of hands, or the power of God. The consensus was that these things went away 2000 years ago and were not active today.

When I returned from college, the first ministry role I participated in was that of usher. Playing my role well, I smiled, escorted people to their seats, and found other ways to make them comfortable.

In retrospect, I understand now that I knew *about* God, but I did not *know* Him. My family was rooted within a particular church, which was a long-held tradition. I went through the motions for years, just like everyone else, putting generational ways above a genuine relationship with God. I did not understand or enter into a relationship with Jesus until I joined an educator's group. Prior to this, my light was darkness, and I was not even aware of it.

Prior to my first meeting of the educator group, I opened my Bible repeatedly to Mark 1: "The time is fulfilled the kingdom of God is at hand. Repent and believe the gospel" (Mark 1:15 NKJV). I did not think I was a bad person, but I knew there was something missing. I needed to take note. When one of my friends in the educator group asked me if I was saved, if I knew Jesus, I had to think about it. I knew deep down something was amiss.

Soon afterwards, I confessed Romans 10: "That if you confess with your mouth the Lord Jesus and believe in your heart that God has raised Him for the dead, you will be saved. For with the heart one believes unto righteousness, and with the mouth confession is made unto salvation" (Rom. 10:9–10 NKJV). I confessed Jesus as my Lord and Savior and have been moving forward since. It was my time and my season. The Word says the sons of Issachar understood the times and seasons (1 Chron. 12:32 author's paraphrase). I believe, when God is nudging us into a new place, we should learn to hear His voice, and obey.

God informs us, in Jeremiah 29: "I know the plans I think toward you says the Lord, thoughts of peace and not of evil, to give you a future and an expected end" (Jer. 29:11 NKJV). God has plans for all of us—even before the foundation of the earth—before we were formed in our mother's womb.

Religion and tradition are no substitute for a relationship with Jesus. God created us to hear His voice and to obey, so that He can have His bidding done throughout the earth. Timothy speaks of a form of godliness, denying the power thereof (2 Tim. 3:5 NKJV). In other words, people may give mental assent but may not have a relationship with God.

Others may get mired down in tradition and (knowingly or unknowingly) substitute those actions for relationships. Mark 7chronicles: "Making the word of God of no effect through your tradition which you have handed down, and many such things you do" (Mark 7:13 KJV). This verse points to valuing tradition, the way my parents or grandfathers did things, regardless of whether the tradition aligns with the Word of God.

Jesus wants us to love Him as He loves us and to give Him our attention. In all of our human effort, we cannot substitute carnal things for true worship. The believer's goal should be to have his spiritual nature gain ascendancy over his natural or carnal nature. A relationship with Jesus causes us to grow and to develop a thirst and hunger for Him. Along the spiritual journey, as we become more aware of Jesus, carnal things diminish in importance.

Jesus is patiently waiting for us to reach "higher" ground. He waits for us to fulfill our purposes and destinies in Him. Jesus knows exactly where each of us is today in our spiritual walk. We may currently demonstrate a lost state, but He's preordained our station and place in Him before we were formed in the womb. We are, in essence, found, but not lost.

God's Homework: You are not lost to God. He knows exactly where you are and is waiting for you to come to Him. Repeat this prayer:

"Father God,

Forgive me of my sins.
I believe in my heart and confess with my mouth
that Jesus Christ is Lord.

I make You my Lord."

33

In the Midst of a Forbidden City—
Lost, But Not Lost

❧

ERNESTINE MEADOWS MAY

What man of you, having a hundred sheep, if he has lost one of them, does not leave the ninety-nine in the open country, and go after the one that is lost, until he finds it? (Luke 15:4 ESV)

There are many stories in the Bible concerning miracles, signs, and wonders where God delivered His people from the ordinary to the pandemic in unprecedented ways! Daniel was thrown into a den of hungry lions, but God was able to lock the jaws of the beasts that delighted in their next meal. God caused the children of Israel to walk through the parting of the Red Sea without the wetness from tons of water that surrounded them. And lest we forget that the three Hebrew boys were cast into a fiery furnace, ordered by King Nebuchadnezzar, because they refused to bow down before him. Our Lord did not balk on a promise made to Sarah that she would bear a child when she was well past her child-bearing age. And remember that little David felled a giant with only a rock and a sling! The same God performed all of these miracles and more! These divine acts of God establish in me a faith and belief that is unshakeable!

I traveled with a delegation of educators led by Mac Brown and sponsored by The Dwight D. Eisenhower Foundation, "People to People," that journeyed to China on a mission of a cultural exchange entitled, "Play in Education." Our base city was Beijing, which has a population of 18.8 million people today. It is the largest city by area and China's capital. We visited the famous Tiananmen Square, the city of Shanghai, and four other cities there. The highlight of our visit was the Forbidden City. It housed the Imperial Palace, which had been the home of twenty-four emperors.

On the morning of our arrival at the gates of the Forbidden City, our tour bus lined the street with other buses that had arrived early as well. We were given instructions as to how we would partner with someone, meet at the bus to go for lunch, and received the usual "stick together and don't get lost" routine. Honestly, I know how to take care of myself in a crowd. I am diligent to observe my surroundings and take note of the street where the bus was parked. I saw that most buses had words written with Chinese characters and our bus had a special mark of identification just for us. So, I was ready to go! And I was extremely excited. I could see the red building in the far distance, beyond the walled borders. I wasn't concerned with many steps ahead because I had been working out prior to the trip and was up for the challenge.

My roommate and I were partners. We all made a detour inside the gates to the souvenir shop. These I love and had only one thought, *"Must have something to show and share when I've returned home."* I got carried away in that shop, and when I looked for the group and my roommate, they had left me alone there. *No problem. I can manage on my own.*

Within an hour, I scanned the grounds and thought to myself, *"Where did all these people suddenly come from?"* No one looked like me. Where is the south gate? Where was the north gate? Where were my people? What time is it? I had heard that we would meet back on the bus at 11 A.M. Or was it noon? I couldn't think! *Pray?* Not in my scared mind! I needed to get back to the bus. I was trying to remember the direction in which I had entered. I knew I saw the Palace in the distance, but was it the front I was looking at or the rear? I just began walking, and thankfully, it was in the direction of a gate where buses were lined on a street. Bumper to bumper, they had lined up everywhere. Tens of thousands more people were involved than when we had arrived and parked. I walked up and down the street but couldn't find our specially labeled bus. No one seemed to speak my language. I certainly did not speak theirs. People from every nation seemed to be here without a single American in sight who could possibly speak English. The bus drivers surveyed me as I ignored their scrutiny. I had a bus to find. After walking for unknown miles, back and forth, I looked up to see that the sky was still blue. That showed me the familiarity of my being! I was not as lost as I had believed.

I prayed upward, "Lord, you know where I am, and I don't want to be lost in a country I know nothing about." Or something like that. I mean, what kind of prayer was that?

Then, an unexplainable peace fell upon me. I let go of my intense feelings. I did not stop walking but slowed my pace. I was not anxious anymore, but copped an attitude of, *"que sera sera"* knowing that somehow whatever will be will be.

I turned and glanced toward the narrow street where I saw a small car driving slowly, the face of the passenger seemed to be staring toward me. The man was waving a red flag. It was obvious that he knew me, but who was *he*? He waved more frantically. I paid attention more markedly. I was found! Found, but not lost from God. He always knew where I was. His angels guided the men to where I was. I had been located out of what seemed a million people. After all, I was *E pluribus Unum* (out of many, one).

God is **Omnipotent** (all-powerful), **Omniscient** (knowing all), and **Omnipresent** (everywhere at the same time). I saw my heavenly Father at work keeping me in His peace until the men he sent to rescue me showed up. If He did it for me, believe that it can happen for you, because He is not a respecter of persons but He is moved by your faith in Him. My God never wants His children to feel that they are lost in any situation. He is always available to us when we rely upon and trust in Him. He is greater than any circumstance. Keep this line from the song, *Amazing Grace* (lyrics by John Newton, 1779), in your heart: "*I once was lost but now I'm found, I was blind but now I see...*"

God's Homework: Consider writing a song to God. Use your own words to the tune of a hymn you already are familiar with.

34

Provision for Promotion

❦

ERNESTINE MEADOWS MAY

*As it is written: No eye has seen, no ear has heard,
no mind had conceived what God has prepared
for those who love Him.* (1 Cor. 2:9 KJV)

From the early days of my teaching career, it seemed that I was always on the lower end of the seniority list when it came to teacher assignments. I thought, since I was hired into the school system, that I would be able to remain in the job until I retired. Well, it did not work out that way. Early hires were at the discretion of being on a need-basis, even past the three years non-tenure status.

I loved teaching kindergarten and wanted to stay in that position forever. Some of us were given notice in the spring that we would not be given a contract for the following year because of low enrollments. Teachers with more seniority could bid for your job if they wanted to. Consequently, I was "bumped" for my position. The first year of teaching really did not faze me very much because I felt at peace about having a job for the next school year. My co-worker was very upset and distraught. She was always talking about it. I remained at peace because I knew God would provide.

I believe that because I trusted Him my needs would be met, I was called to fill a position at another school offering better materials and working conditions, along with a friendly staff and very cooperative parents with well-behaved students. The test scores were the highest of most schools in the city. When it's time for you to become uprooted or transplanted, keep an open mind and consider that, when one door closes, God will and can rearrange things for your benefit. He will open doors that you did not see for yourself. He knows the ending from the beginning.

I bounced around from grade level to grade level, while other teachers remained in their same classrooms. For me though, change was good. It gave me the opportunity to become familiar with different teaching styles and strategies according to the level of the students. I was later offered an opportunity to travel to China and Africa on teacher exchange programs at the expense of the school system. I received training and certification in Montessori Methods through the generosity of our school, and with their cooperation I was able to participate in the newly formed Early Childhood Development Center. I applied for and was hired as a facilitator to help monitor and promote successful achievement for all students. I was given an opportunity to apply for and be hired as the principal of the Early Childhood Development Center, which was the only established one of its kind in the State of Indiana at that time.

God had me! I was a living example of Jeremiah 29: "I know the plan I have for you, declares the Lord. A plan that will prosper and not harm you, plans to give you hope and future" (Jer. 29:11 KJV).

God's Homework: Create a vision board that represents to the world that you have a BIG GOD! Represent your career path, spiritual growth, relationships, and other hopes and dreams.

35

Giving and Provision

~

SHELLEY M. FISHER, PH.D.

Honor the Lord with your possessions, and with the
first fruits of all your increase. (Prov. 3:10 NKJV)

I believe that tithing and the giving of offerings always work for our good. Malachi 3 says, "Bring ye all the tithes in the storehouse, that there may me meat in my house and prove me now therewith, saith the Lord of hosts, if I will not open you the windows of heaven, and pour you out a blessing, that there shall not be room enough to receive it. And I will rebuke the devour for your sake…" (Mal. 3:10–11a KJV). As Christians, we traditionally identify this verse with giving ten percent of our income back to God in some way. However, Luke 6 says, "Give and it will be given to you, A good measure, pressed down, shaken together and running over, will be poured into your lap. For with the measure you use, it will be measured to you" (Luke 6:38 NIV). Note that there is no limit. You may receive some thirty, sixty, or one hundred percent in return.

One notable provision memory came to my mind as I executed my own paying of tithes and offerings. Both of my children were in college; my family's finances were squeezed tight; and I needed a new vehicle. Even with my husband's and my incomes, it seemed impossible. I could see no logical way our needs could be met.

The teacher's credit union sent a notification that they were having a car sale, supported by a local car renting/leasing company. A few days later, I was coming from the grocery store and remembered the sale being held a few blocks away. I saw no harm in going by just to look. When I walked into the rental/leasing company, it was as if an agent had been waiting for me. I told him I wanted to look around, but that I was not interested in purchasing anything. I had not even discussed the idea with my husband.

Nevertheless, he started showing me vehicles that were slightly used, had low mileage, but were, actually, the present year models. I saw one car that I really liked. The agent asked me to sit in the vehicle and started explaining its many features.

Then, he said, "Why don't you take it for a spin around the block?"

I thought to myself, "*This guy really thinks I am going to buy something, and I don't have any money.*"

After driving only a few blocks, I fell in love with the car. When I returned to the office the agent was ending a phone call.

He said, "I was just talking to your credit union. I told them I wanted you to take this vehicle with you today."

I explained that was not possible due to the fact that I had not talked with my husband about purchasing a vehicle. He suggested I take the vehicle with me and keep it for the weekend, saying "You and your husband come see me on Monday."

I did just that. On Monday, my husband and I returned to the company to complete the paperwork. No money exchanged hands and I had a new vehicle that was affordable through the transaction with my credit union. God is faithful. He always meets you where you are. He met me and orchestrated a deal that was amenable to my situation and finances at the time.

Many people use the Old Testament verse from Malachi 3 to govern their tithing or lack thereof: "Bring all of the tithes in the storehouse and prove now herewith if I will not open the windows of heaven and pour you out a blessing you will be unable to receive." It continues, "I will rebuke the devour for your sake" (Mal. 3:10

KJV). When you give your tithes, the Lord, Himself, will keep the devil at bay. Some counter that this Scripture is not for today; that we are not to live under the Old Testament. But I disagree.

The Lord places various people in our paths to help us and to get us to the place where He wants us. While in the educator's group, I started to listen to and follow a Bible teacher on television, Marilyn Hickey. She shared that she and her husband were in need of a new car. She said their car was in such bad shape that they did not know if it would get them to their next meeting. She and her husband had saved money. I think about $2,000. While in a church meeting, her husband put all of their savings into the offering. He told his wife that he believed the Lord had told him to do so.

Within a few weeks, a pastor came to their church. He said the Lord had told him that they needed a car and he felt led to take up an offering for them to get one. They received the necessary funds. On the day I watched her tell of this incident, she also stated that the Lord had given her an anointing to pray for people who needed cars. I had called her prayer line and asked for prayer. I then received the blessing to get the car that I needed.

The New Testament talks about giving in Luke 6:38. You can give to receive, and God definitely makes a way when there seems to be no way possible. He is a supernatural God. He can move by His Spirit in your life. He wants us to give a portion of our earnings, talents, and time for the work of the ministry. Giving is an important part of kingdom building. Jesus gave of Himself, as He walked the earth doing good, healing the sick, feeding the poor, and teaching in the temple. As He gave, so should we. In return, giving brings return and increase to every aspect of life.

God's Homework: Do you tithe and give offerings? If you are to prosper and align with God's will, you must give because our Savior gave liberally and continues to shower us with His blessings. Examine yourself in light of the Word that deals with giving. Give that you might advance the kingdom.

36

The House Worth Thousands

SHELLEY M. FISHER, PH.D.

The blessing of the Lord makes one rich...
(Prov. 10:22 NKJV)

I received a call from my husband telling me about a realtor we knew who was trying to interest him in buying a house. We would be able to pay pennies on the dollar of what the house was worth by simply paying the back taxes due. He had already told the realtor that he was not interested, but to call his wife—who likes to do that stuff. That would be me. He further told me to expect the call.

I was familiar with the house. It was near my husband's family home: a three-bedroom, brick, with a fireplace, basement, and garage. The realtor called to let me know that the taxes were indeed unpaid, but at the last minute the bank had made the decision to put the house on the county auction foreclosure list. He gave me the number of the property. The tax amount was $2,300.

I scurried to the county government building and found the auction auditorium with the identification number that the realtor had given me. I had never attended a foreclosure auction but had formed my real estate investment limited license company and bought one short sale property from a bank. This was the extent of my real estate experience.

When the property came up, I bid on it. Another guy was bidding as well. I outbid him by $500 and the property was ours. I bought a $100,000 property for $2,800! I was not looking for a property, and I knew nothing about foreclosures, nor bidding. The house literally "fell in my lap." I had my team renovate the kitchen and bathroom, remove the carpeting, and refinish the hardwood floors. The house continues to provide residual income for me today.

The Word says that you, the believer, will get houses that you did not build. The Lord also says that no man, who has left houses, brothers or sisters or father and mother, for His sake will fail to receive a hundredfold in return. (Deut. 6:11; Matt.19:29 NKJV). God honors our tithing and offerings beyond anything we can imagine.

God's Homework: When you give tithes and offerings, blessings "chase" you. You do not tell God how to bless you. He looks for ways to bless you when you are in relationship with Him. He is more than willing and able to pour you out a blessing you will not have room enough to receive (Luke 6:38 author's paraphrase). The law of sowing and reaping is at work in our life; so when you give, expect to receive.

37

A Gift Delayed—
But Not Denied

~✕~

GLORIA SHARPE SMITH

*Delight thyself in the Lord, and he will give thee
the desires of thine heart.* (Ps. 37:4 KJV)

It was mid-morning when I walked the short distance from my front door to the mailbox. I held, in my hand, a very creative piece of art that had been skillfully crafted into a delightful birthday card. The words "Happy Birthday" were cut out in the shape of buildings of various heights and colors. They popped up when the card was opened to be read. All of this was fashioned on lightweight card stock. While browsing the Internet, I had gone to the Lovepop.com website and selected this particular card for one, very special person: my son. The design was unique. I knew he would appreciate it as much as I did. My very first Lovepop card had come from him.

Since the card was for his fifty-first birthday, I decided to add a little something special. I went to the bank and requested one crisp $50 bill and a crisp $100 bill; both were going into the card. My thinking was that the fifty would represent five decades of his life and the hundred, the one year; thus, his age. I was well aware that putting cash in the mail was not a wise thing to do, but a check for that amount would not have the same visual impact. I was going for creativity. Plus, I knew if I sent a check, it would never get cashed. This was all about art, creativity, thoughtfulness, and making a general fuss for his birthday. I carefully added the finishing touch of my handwritten message: *"Happy 51st Birthday to my talented, creative, and loving son. From your loving, always thinking of ways to make you smile, Mom."*

As I placed the card in my mailbox, I raised the red flag on the side to alert the mail carrier of its presence. Just when most everyone might be thinking all would be well, I got an uneasy feeling in the pit of my stomach. And, even though no human was around, I heard a gentle whisper in my ear that said, *"You should not put cash in the mail."* I acknowledged the feeling and the voice that stopped me dead in my tracks. I responded with a simple prayer that went something like this: "Father, thank You for blessing me to be able to send this to Tony. I'm trusting You to get it safely to him for his birthday on October 2nd. I am not going to fear because of what's going on with the mail system right now. Thank You for getting it there safely. In Jesus' Name." That settled it all for me. I went on about my day.

I didn't think anything else about the card, the money, or the mail system until October 2. I called to wish my son a happy birthday and to tell him to check his PO Box for mail. Since I had mailed the card eight days earlier, and had double-checked the address, I was certain that it would be there waiting for him. He thanked me for sending something and said that he would get it.

About two weeks later, we spoke again. My son had not gone to his P.O. Box yet, because of the Covid-19 stay-at-home restrictions that were in place in Los Angeles. Furthermore, he reminded me that his P.O. Box was quite a distance from his home. I understood that. However, I confess to being a little frustrated because I knew that he was going to really appreciate the uniqueness of the card's design and the generous, creative idea behind "Fifty-One." For him, it would be a positive vibe and I wanted him to have it. My patience was being tested.

Fast forward to October 29: Another two weeks had passed before I received a call from him.

"Mom, there's no mail in my box from you."

My stomach dropped and my mouth got instantly dry! What did I hear the voice say? *"Gloria, you should not have put that money in the mail!"*

I said to my son, "Did you ask the clerk if perhaps they have taken mail out of your box? Could they have put it someplace else for you, since you haven't been there in a while; and with everything else that's going on with Covid?"

He said, "No, I've had the box for over twenty years, and nothing has ever been missing."

I was speechless! All kinds of thoughts started to run through my mind. *"Gloria you should have taken it to the post office. You should have sent it certified mail. Why didn't he go to pick it up before now? Well, did it ever leave Texas? I don't know! Anyway, Lord, I trusted you to* get it *safely to him and he does not have it!"*

But that small, unsettling voice had cautioned me as I walked away from my mailbox after I had placed the card there. My emotions were all over the place. I was very disappointed. I was upset with my son because it had taken him too long, in my opinion, to go to the box. The entire ordeal was a big letdown for me. My son remarked that he was sorry the card wasn't there, but maybe whoever got it needed it more. He was "okay" with that. I tried to feel the same way, however, deep down inside I really didn't. I felt that God had let me down. My son didn't understand just how important it was to me that he had that particular birthday card. Eventually, I got over it and didn't think about it anymore. I accepted the fact that he knew I had thought about him. He had let it go and I had to do the same.

Some weeks later, I was involved in a Zoom meeting with a group of ladies and I noticed a striking black and gold throw being used as a background with the words "Roosevelt Panthers" emblazoned on it. I inquired about it and learned that the school's alumni club was selling them. My son is an alumni of Roosevelt High School, where he had been an outstanding Panther. I ordered a throw for him and had it mailed to my home. After it arrived, I drove around with it in my car for several weeks before finally taking it to the post office on December twenty-third. I was not trying to get it to him as a Christmas gift, so the date really didn't matter. I mailed it to the same P.O. Box as the illusive card. *This* time, I took a picture of the mailing label and texted it to him, as an alert that a package was on the way. He inquired as to what I was sending.

I simply texted back, "Surprise!"

He asked, "Why didn't you mail it to my house?"

I responded, "Because you always told me to send mail to your box!"

His response was, "Mom, that was before Covid. The box is *quite* a ways from where I live, and I don't get out on a regular basis."

Once again, I thought, *this is not going well!* I shipped the package through FedEx and it had a scheduled delivery date of December 30. I passed this information along, with the hope that he would go promptly to the box this time to retrieve the package. I also felt it was my responsibility to let him know when I received the notification from FedEx that the package had been delivered as scheduled.

Once again, I was in a heightened mode of anticipation concerning his reaction. Over the years, he's always shown great appreciation for the gifts I've given him. He tells me we are on the same wavelength, and I quite enjoy hearing that. I had the rare pleasure of exceeding all of these emotions on December 31. On the last day of 2020, the text I received will always remain unforgettable. I was totally unprepared for pictures of the September 25th post-marked envelope that contained the birthday card with all of the cash still securely in place, along with the black and gold Roosevelt throw! Here were all of his gifts and my answered prayers!

The accompanying message said, "The lesson here is to never give power to the things we can't control and that only get us upset."

My response, "God is faithful, and His word is true. I learned a lesson and my confidence in what I believe is strengthened. I'm glad you have all that was intended for you! That was my prayer and it's been answered. I'm dancing with joy because one of my favorite Scriptures is Psalms 37:4 which says, "Delight yourself in the Lord and he will give you the desires of your heart." Well, my heart's desire was for you to have the birthday card with the cash and the throw. You have them both, I am grateful."

Our conversation reminded me of the rest of the message that I had written to him in the card:

But blessed is the one who trusts in the Lord, whose confidence is in him." — Jeremiah 17:7

Blessings for another great year. Happy Birthday, Son
I Love you!! Mom

I soon came to realize that I had received a very special gift through this ordeal, a stronger faith in the Word of God. It's one thing to read the Bible and the stories of those who have gone before us, but there's nothing like having your very own personal experience. I was elated and grateful for both the grace and the faithfulness that had been shown to me. God encourages us to do so. "But without faith it is impossible to please him, for he that cometh to God must believe that he is, and that he is a rewarder of them that diligently seek him" (Heb. 11:6 KJV).

There came a calm whisper into my ear saying, "*You walked away from the mailbox and said,* 'I'm trusting you to get it to him safely.' *I heard your prayer and honored your faith.*" I don't always hear those whispers. Sometimes, life is so busy; I miss them. Gratitude filled my heart because of His faithfulness.

The very next text message that I opened contained these words: "You shall end this year in JOY in Jesus' name."

And that's exactly what happened!

God's Homework: Embrace a disappointing situation with hope for a desirable outcome. Write your expected outcome on a card or in your journal.

38

Giving Triggers Giving

AS TOLD TO ERNESTINE MEADOWS MAY
BY HER SISTER, LOUISE MEADOWS CALDWELL

Give and it shall be given unto you, good measure,
pressed down and shaken together shall men give
unto your bosom. (Luke 6:38 KJV)

If you would like to be affected by a charge or change in your life, open your heart to what is unexplainable, and see the world through the eyes of a believer in Christ Jesus, rather than through natural eyes. You will not be able to find these kinds of miracles in a textbook. Many people believe they are responsible by themselves for overcoming situations, achieving successes, or making their moves up the ladders of financial bliss. In reality, God reigns over the just as well as the unjust. In order to extend His hand to the believer, the move may require touching someone else as a result.

Change your thinking and you can change your place of being!

My sister, Louise, is so blessed by the Lord. She does not go about loudly proclaiming how great she is, but in following her life, one could well see how grace and mercy have been her companions all of the days of her life.

We were raised in the same household with a prayerful mother, a mother obedient to the Word of God. And this has played out in different ways concerning her children. Louise has always been a giver, helper, and lover of people. She is always in a good place with people, and willing to stand in wherever she fits. She told me of a time that she really needed a job and had applied at a well-known electronic factory some years ago. Our sister, Mae, was the line inspector supervisor at the plant in Chicago, Illinois. The job required her to be able to work on an assembly line and solder circuit board wiring for televisions, stereos, and transistor radios according to specifications.

"Well, I didn't know a thing about how to do this work, but I needed this job," she stated. "One day, while working on the line, I had to prove my ability to retain the job at this factory."

She couldn't ask our sister, who was her supervisor, because it would show favoritism. Doing so might create some fallout complaints regarding nepotism. Louise was the second person on the assembly line, so the process was dependent upon her to keep the line moving by performing her job and keeping the work pieces moving along the line, performing at a predetermined level of speed and accuracy. Her line boss came out to observe. He was met with a work stoppage at the far end of the line.

He yelled out, "What's going on here? Why isn't this line moving?"

He confronted Louise to let her know that she had one more chance to perform the work as it should be done. During her break, she stayed on the line to try and get caught up. Then she went to the bathroom and prayed as she had never done before. She confessed to me that something happened in that restroom. She felt a confidence rise in her as she returned back to the floor and began putting together circuit boards and soldering the right wires to the corresponding links with little or no effort on her part. God had heard her prayer and she was able to continue on as a successful assembly line employee.

Know that God hears and answers your prayers. When you are in a desperate situation, it calls for desperate measures. If life seems to push you into a corner, push back with the Word of God in prayer.

When you give to others and do good by them, God remembers. He will compensate you for your good. The Bible tells us so in 2 Corinthians 9: "You will be enriched in every way so that you can be generous on every occasion, and through your generosity will result in thanksgiving to God" (2 Cor. 9:11 NIV). Our job is to believe that it is so.

God's Homework: Have a conversation with a family member, friend, or acquaintance. Ask them about an on-the-job problem and find out how it was solved. Think about how you would have reacted if it had been your problem. If you currently have a challenge at work, share it with someone today.

39

Who's Your Momma?

❦

ERNESTINE MEADOWS MAY

Never have I seen the righteous forsaken or his
seed begging for bread. (Ps. 37:2 ASV)

It hurt my heart to tears to come home from college and see my momma in the field on hot summer days, chopping cotton. I did not like this life for her. I vowed that when I was able, I would help her out of the situation. I was the last child walking. She looked so abandoned, but I just had to keep on trekking to reach my goal of completing a college education. She was the oldest of seven sisters and brothers plus, after her father remarried there were four more additional siblings in the family. She had to drop out of school when her mother died to make sure everyone was cared for.

My older siblings had all left after high school to find their stations in life. It was very hard to leave my mother on the farm to manage things on her own, but I knew she wanted this for me as much as I wanted it for myself. Times were changing.

Momma was always a praying woman. Her faith was set. As far back as I can remember, she attended church every Saturday evening and Tuesday Bible study and sewing circle with the church ladies. Sundays were church-oriented all day long starting with early morning Sunday school, mid-day services, and in evenings it was YPWW for the kids, then regular evening services that would last into the wee hours of the morning. She never missed a beat nor complained but gave of her time and volunteered before God to be of service to Him.

In spite of all of this church activity, a country breakfast and a bountiful dinner would be prepared for our pastor and his family of six. No one made smothered chicken, falling off the bone, like she did or that yummy butter roll floating in an ice cream custard, nicely browned and hot from the oven. This was the routine every weekend because our church pastor came in on weekends from another city. She provided a likeness of today's Bed and Breakfast services when there was no such thing to be had in our small town. The two blended families of twelve came together without stress, complaint, or discord. My sisters and I gave up our room. Two full beds and a foldable rolling cot were added to accommodate living arrangements. We took a palate to the living room floor. It was fun. My older sister, Louise, was a scary storyteller and she entertained us well.

My momma was a very industrious woman. She made sure that we had enough provisions to feed our family. We had a consistent diet of every vegetable that would be planted in a two-acre garden, pecan trees, along with an orchard of peaches, pears, plums, and apples that had been planted by my daddy. She canned enough food to take us throughout the winter months and would give much more to our neighbors. She cured venison. It was my job to churn milk curds to make butter. I hated that job, but loved the cakes, rolls and pies that resulted. We raised cattle, chickens, hogs, and goats.

Because of her willingness to share with others, the windows of heaven opened up to her, the grounds opened up to yield the strength of the ground. It was her sixty-fold return of all that she had given. We had a great supply of provisions because of her willingness to share out of her abundance and give to the church of her tithes and offerings. God honored His Word as it states in Malachi 3: "'test Me now…,' says the LORD of hosts, 'If I will not open for you the windows of heaven and pour out for you a blessing until it overflows'" (Mal. 3:10 NASB).

I remember when our pastor called on the membership to make a pledge of $200 for the church building fund—a new church was greatly needed. My momma was one of the first to make that pledge. In those days, a hundred dollars was like a thousand bucks today. I was thinking, *"Where will she get that kind of money?"* We had plenty of supplies, but that wasn't in money! She and her friend, Mrs. Evelyn, had a plan. They were excellent cooks, so they decided to sell dinners on Saturdays and desserts of homemade ice cream as an extra special treat. It wasn't long before they had profited from the project to the tune of two hundred dollars apiece.

Momma made the things that she did seem easy. I think she invented the "Easy Button" somewhere along the process of living this life of promise. She trusted her God and He delivered. She labored for the "rest" and was rewarded with so many resulting desires of her heart.

One of my earlier goals was reached when God blessed us, as three of her daughters, and a granddaughter, were able to purchase a home for her in the little town in which we had lived and grown up. We wanted her to be able to walk to church around the corner every Sunday to fellowship along with her friends. She had lived in the country for most of her life, working very hard. Her health was not as strong as it once was. However, she was blessed in the country and now blessed in the city. Everyone knew my momma as a loving, kind, generous, humble and a Godly woman.

I learned a lot from her—and her ways. She was the foundation of my person. Because of her giving, God provided for her in abundance. Because of her prayers, God has honored and blessed her seed. It would be a very sad commentary to know that someone's name has never been called out to God in prayer. This is the way of the intercessor, to be mediator, to be one who pleads on behalf of another. Many nights I peeked into my momma's room to see her kneeled in prayer. I know that God heard her desperate pleas to bless us and keep us. He did! Her actions remind me of Matthew 5: *"Blessed are the meek, for they shall inherit the earth, (kingdom of God)"* (Matt. 5:5 KJV).

God's Homework: Text, call, or write your mother and let her know that one great thing that you appreciate her for. If you do not have a mother, choose another female figure who has inspired you.

40

A Pandemic Move

⌒✕⌒

SHELLEY M. FISHER, PH.D.

But those who hope in the LORD will renew their strength.
They will soar on wings like eagles; they will run and not grow
weary; they will walk and not be faint. (Isa. 40:31 KJV)

In the pandemic I held onto my faith. There were moments when I wondered where the spiritual leaders, preachers, evangelists, pastors, and teachers had gone, *"Where is the voice of the prophets?"* I wanted them to get airtime and tell the world that all was well; God was still at the helm and victory was ours. The silence of our leaders was deafening.

When they finally did speak, some of the renowned prophets that I'd held in high esteem said nothing about the coronavirus. Additionally, their comments were conflicting. The Word of the Lord, told to me, was to keep my eyes on Him and He would give me perfect peace. This continues to be my solace.

God is calling us to lead in the space where we are, to be His mouthpiece and to be calm in the midst of the storm. I am grateful that God is the same—yesterday, today, and forevermore. He is not daunted, or sullied by anything that is going on. He knew about this virus before the foundation of the earth. I believe His voice is saying to us, "The kingdom of God is being fulfilled. Repent and believe the gospel" (Mark 15:1 NKJV).

Some things and certain situations just dwarf us. They are no match for us. It is times like these when we should let go, casting our imaginations and every high thing on the Lord. He says His yoke is easy and His burden is light. We are to cast all of our cares upon Him. What a consolation to know that we have a burden bearer who stands ready to take our cares upon Himself, for He is more than able to handle our concerns.

God's remedy for present times is to pray for those in authority (1 Tim. 2:1–2). Pray for wisdom, knowledge, counsel, might, and that the fear of the Lord would rest upon leadership. Also pray that God, holding the heart of the king in His hands, will turn the heart of leadership toward Himself. We cannot look to mankind for we are disconcerting and filled with blatant wrongs, going unaddressed. But our God sits high and looks low. He will not be mocked. Keep your eyes on Him where victory lies.

The Word says to speak to the mountain, and it will be cast into the sea. Faith, tenacity, and perseverance in prayer will bring us through these dismal days. My hope lies in the Word of the Lord. God's wisdom dispels foolishness, narcissism, and stupidity. God always has a remnant of the faithful among us and stays ready to receive our repentance and to reconcile us to Himself.

I thank God for His sovereignty and His prevailing love and power to achieve His will on the earth. One of my favorite verses is: "For the Lord God is a Sun and a Shield. For the Lord will give grace and glory. No good thing will he withhold from those walking uprightly" (Ps. 84:11 NKJV). When days or situations are dreary, Jesus is the sun, shining brightly. When danger is lurking in hidden places, He is a shield and a protector. As long as you walk uprightly, attend to His Word, and live by His precepts, not only will He give grace and glory, but He will not withhold good things from us. God is an awesome God, ever mindful of us. He is a rewarder of those who diligently seek Him. Who would not serve a God like this?

As believers, we do not have to fret and fear anything. When we are in relationship with God, He is our protector, shield, buckler, high tower and dwelling place. He is to us whatever we need Him to be. We can rest from the storm and ill winds wreaking havoc. There is a confidence that the believer has that it is well, no matter what it may look like, seem like, or feel like. When cultivated, a relationship with God is an umbrella of safety and victory.

God's Homework: Are you hidden in God? Do you remember Him when things are not going well? Remember to keep your focus on Him and He promises to keep you in perfect peace. Deliberately use the Word when going through challenges. Hide the promises in your heart: "The righteous cry out, and the Lord hears, and delivers them out of all their troubles" (Ps. 34:7 NKJV).

41

A Pandemic Moment

***

SHELLEY M. FISHER, PH.D.

The Lord on high is mightier, than the noise of many waters,
than the mighty waves of the sea. (Ps. 93:4 NKJV)

In the month of February 2020, the nation was still getting information about the pandemic. The news media reported on China and its activities, and on wearing masks. Americans viewed the virus as unlikely to travel here. We were still in the observation stage because we had not been mandated to wear masks yet.

The progression was familiar to me, because my husband had undergone successful back surgery and was transferred to another hospital for physical therapy. His nurse was someone I knew who believed in the power of God. She took good care of him. During this time, hospital visitation was unpredictable. At unpredictable times, visitors would be asked to leave. Soon, upon entering, the guard in the lobby took temperatures. The virus did not seem to be so far away at this point.

Then we began to hear of people dying and hospitals becoming overcrowded with Covid-19 patients. My husband's release was welcomed. The facility's visitation hours were sporadic. I had already overheard nurses speaking of a deluge of incoming Covid-19 patients to our hospital.

The Center for Disease Control (CDC) and Dr. Fauci began to request people wear masks. I had a new granddaughter I was not able to see, nor were my children visiting my husband and I. The gravity of the situation was setting in. Businesses and restaurants began closing and a deepening reality of the seriousness of the situation was becoming evident.

Then it happened. Churches closed, set limits, or mandated that no more than nine people should attend funerals. Parking lot preaching and Facebook Live became the order of church services. My pastor shared his "pulpit" with me. Parking lot preaching was a way to continue to get the Word out. Congregants stayed in their cars as I peached. If something resonated with them, horns started honking—a new expressive way of voicing "Amen" or "Hallelujah." Communion was held in the parking lot as well. People from the neighborhood began to come out on their porches to listen to the services. For those who did not attend the parking lot service, a video was set up so they could view the service from home.

Preaching to empty pews and taping the service via Facebook was another experience. God was hovering over me in those services as well. It was common practice to watch once-filled churches on television now empty. The gospel must be preached regardless of adverse circumstances. To me it is with humility and gratitude that I celebrated being God's spokesperson. I am blessed that my pastor was amenable to sharing the "pulpit." The food pantry became a drive-through giveaway with vehicles slowing down and workers putting the food in trunks while maintaining social distance. We do what must be done.

Technology helped to advance the kingdom during the pandemic. We found we could preach, teach, and minister to people in the safety of their homes or vehicles. God's creativity was even shown through the days of church closings. I never could have imagined my days of preaching in the parking lot or to empty pews. God's Word accomplished the thing for which it was sent. It is such an honor to be in the service of the Lord, while adjusting and manipulating circumstances for the safety of the people. To God be the glory!

God's Homework: There is nothing too difficult for God. Are you able to adapt during adverse times? Do you mumble and explain about how things used to be in better times? With God we can adapt and adjust and still receive His Word. He makes a way when doors close. Keep your focus on God and avail yourself to His bounty.

42

Unspeakable Joy

❧

GLORIA SHARPE SMITH

*I have no greater joy than to hear that my
children walk in truth.* (3 John 1:4 KJV)

My son introduced me to a young woman who was beautiful, intelligent, artistic, and witty. Sheree was a delight to be around, and I quickly came to admire her. She was an amazing single mom, who also happened to have the luxury of retaining a housekeeper who assisted her with the care of her young son, along with the added bonus of both her mother and grandmother to make a loving fuss over him. I considered them to be a spectacular family unit. Over time, we began to spend many enjoyable moments together. I got to know them all very well; however, there was always one concern lurking in the back of my mind, continually flirting with my heart. It was their relationships with God. I wondered about it, "*Did they each have one?*" I began praying faithfully for such a relationship to occur and was committed to showing them God's love unconditionally.

Early in the friendship, I learned that she didn't own a Bible. That was not good and didn't sit well with me. Evidently the Lord agreed because, after one of my visits, upon returning home, the Holy Spirit instructed me to purchase a Bible and mail it to her. I had no idea how she would receive it, or if she would ever want to discuss anything pertaining to it with me. I just prayed and obeyed.

I didn't hear anything from her regarding the most precious gift that she could have ever received, but the Bible did not come back to me. I didn't mention it and neither did she.

Eventually, I went back to LA and visited with her. We attended a church service together. I was hopeful that she would become a regular attendee. She was showing interest in spirituality and I was pleased. My prayer was always for her to become acquainted with Jesus. I soon learned that she had been reading her Bible and was acquiring a hunger for spiritual matters. God was up to something that I knew nothing about. I felt as though, somehow, this was a setup for her to get what she needed to get to where He was leading.

Sheree's interest in spiritual matters kept growing. They were evidenced when she showed interest in attending a women's conference in New Orleans. I was thrilled when she contacted me and extended the invitation. She made all the arrangements. I had great expectations for a wonderful experience.

It didn't work out that way. I attended all of the sessions at the conference alone. She had an excuse daily for not joining me. The first day she was sleepy and had jet lag because of the time change. The second day, she wasn't feeling well and was "just plain tired." I didn't understand how someone could be so full of enthusiasm about attending a conference of such notoriety and not go to one single session. It was beyond any logic. It certainly appeared as if this was not going to be a time for spiritual bonding. I still held onto my hopes and continued to pray for God's presence in her life. I prayed for favor and blessings that she would grow and find the answer to what His plan was for her. At the very least, she was searching and seeking. That was a joy to behold.

As she grew spiritually, we attended other women's conferences and talked more about spiritual matters. Our time together was something very special to me. The change in her was noticeable. God was answering prayer.

One time we attended a conference in Ohio. She was singled out for prayer by a well-known minister who prayed over her fervently. It was an amazing experience for both of us. It had now become obvious that she was serious about her new life in Christ. She was reading her Bible and actively growing her faith.

Over the years I've witnessed how she became the light in her family. Her daily life reflected her love for God and others. She became very influential in her family's spiritual growth and encouraged them in their faith. She still honors me as her spiritual mother. For that, I'm grateful, but the credit truly belongs to our Lord. I've learned that God always has a plan for our lives. We just need to be diligent in seeking Him to discover it. We can't always see what the outcome will be when we meet an individual and a relationship develops. Yet, I have been richly blessed by following through with Sheree. I call her my Ree Ree. My heart dances with joy each time I am allowed to know about or participate in experiences of God's favor and grace upon her life. These days, she expresses her love for the Word of God through recordings of Scriptures and prayers, which she sets to music.

We may think certain prayers take a long time to be answered; however, it's always a moment of great joy to witness God at work and to see prayer bear fruit. It's been years now since God blessed me with Sheree. I still get misty-eyed when she shares her heart with me in excitement over her position of having God's grace and favor. I have no idea how many lives have been touched through *her* corresponding acts of obedience and consistent prayer. God positioned me, back then, to connect with a young woman who He had need of. He has gone on to bless her life in service to others, demonstrating an undeniable passion for Him and His Word.

Clean Heart

by Sheree Zampino

*Now to him who is able to do immeasurably more
than all we ask or imagine, according to his power
that is at work within us.* (Eph. 3:20 NIV)

Father, I thank you that we all have what we need in you and
that you are the giver and supplier of all good things. You are
a God of abundance and the God of more than enough. I'm
praying that our minds catches up with our reality, oh God, and
that we are able to see from an abundance and gain perspective
versus one where we're focused on our lack and just our needs.
I am praying that we aren't so hyper-focused on ourselves, but
that we are connected to your plan and your purposes for our
life; that we will honor each other, that we will bear each other's
burdens.

God, deliver us from a poverty mentality, a mindset that thinks
there's not enough to go around, a way of thinking that con-
siders me and mine and that puts my brother and sister in direct
competition with me. Father forgive us for competing with
those we are called to love, forgive us for hoarding, oh God.
Forgive us for withholding, forgive us for being afraid to reach
out and to reach back. Deal with us, God. Create in us a clean
heart; a heart that is pure, that seeks to accomplish our God-
given assignment. Deliver us from being pressured with ourselves to the point we condemn and always point out our flaws.

You said in your word that Satan is the accuser of the brethren. I
rebuke and deal with the thoughts and mindsets that think it's
okay to dwell on the faults or the flaws of others' mindsets and
critical spirits that always point out the shortcomings in ourselves and in others. Father, let us lay aside every weight and the

sin which so easily ensnares and let us run with endurance the race that is set before us, looking unto Jesus, the author and the finisher of our faith. Deliver us from oppressive thoughts and influences. I bind the atmosphere. I take authority over every plot, plan, and assignment that the enemy has meant to enslave us and to keep us from our true and intended self. Empower us to make faith decisions versus those rooted in fear. I declare and I decree that we will speak life over each other; that we will let ourselves off the hook, forgiving ourselves.

Father, I thank you for our righteousness that you imputed in us, a righteousness that we cannot earn. I ask that you convict us, Holy Spirit, every time we try to make ourselves earn something through our behavior. We are saved by grace and not of works, let us rest in the knowing of your grace.

Lord, give us supernatural revelation that we don't work to gain what you so freely give us. You came to set the captives free. Oh God, I pray for revelation of the truth about who we are and what you think of us. If we only knew; if we only knew and believed.

Father, deal with our issues of self-entitlement. Lord, they are rooted in fear and self-pity. I pray for a true and positive self-image. I'm not who they said I am! I am who you say I am! Lord, we are created in your image; we are crowned with glory and with honor. We are not to live defeated and discouraged but to reign and rule in authority which you have given.

Our weapons are mighty for tearing down strongholds. We have the tools necessary to defeat any obstacle and to deal with any hindrance. We are well-equipped and we are well able. We will be anxious for nothing; we won't worry about anything; but we will pray about everything! Lord, we will tell you what we need and thank and praise you in advance.

God, we praise you just because you're God. We will place our cares, concerns, our heartbreaks and desires at your feet and then leave room for your sovereignty, oh God.

I pray that you teach us to be content in whatsoever situation we find ourselves, because your grace is certainly sufficient. Your grace is sufficient.

Father, fill our hearts with understanding, so that we can declare with a heart filled with gratitude that it is well with my soul. It is well with my soul!

Note: Scripture quoted from various translations of the Bible.

God's Homework: Follow through with anything you believe the Lord has asked you to do— even if it seems crazy!

43

Kingdom Giving Expands the Kingdom

ERNESTINE MEADOWS MAY

Fear not little flock, it is your father's good pleasure to give you the kingdom. (Luke 12:32 KJV)

Keep in mind that God can and will turn, for His use in the kingdom, what you desire. I am remembering school students I've hosted as Cultural Exchange Students from countries such as Colombia, Belgium, Germany, Brazil, Taiwan, France, and Japan. These students were sent by order and design. I was to be the conduit for their exposure and experiences, hopefully resulting in each of them making educated choices that would affect life decisions down the road. I was up for the challenge because I was a solicitor of culturally based knowledge. I was also aware of what would be needed of me: patience, respect for differences, and understanding. My hope was that I didn't fail too much in those areas. Love was easy. It came naturally for me because I wanted to please God always. It is because of His love for me that I am able to, in return, love others.

I tried to expose the students to some activities and happenings from an American point of view. A year passes really fast and sometimes all of the lists of things to do are not realized, but I always enjoyed the sharing!

The greatest reward from these experiences came from a student from Taiwan who continues to express her gratitude for our connection (which I believe was divinely of God). She was feisty and strong willed, Maggi, from Taiwan. All of our students attended church with us on Sundays. It was not required but the invitation was extended. One never knows what impact or influence a person, experience, or thing may extract from an extended hand. I really missed all of our exchange students when they left. Each had unique personalities. They were very respectful, obedient, courteous, and genuine in their appreciation of the opportunity for the exchange. I'm sure we learned more from them than they did from us. They came to this country with a knowledge of history and an expectation of the life that they had observed from social media and by way of movies and television. Maggi still remembers us at different holidays, especially Christmas, and always includes a note of thanksgiving. When her year was up in the States, she returned home, finished college, and secured a visa to return and work here. She has settled in the Eastern U.S. and is working for a well-known financial brokerage company.

But that is not the particular story I wanted to share about Maggi. While a student here she was joined into the kingdom of God at our church in Chicago, Illinois, by water baptism. Her testimony is a wonderful one of salvation. She continues to pray for her entire family to become believers in our Lord and Savior, Jesus Christ.

She has expressed that living with us during that year caused her to do things for herself, rather than allowing me to do everything for her. Those actions, in turn, helped her to become the strong and independent young lady that she is today. That was my philosophy in raising my own children, "learn by doing." That's how God takes the simple to confound the wise! Taiwan has a history of worshiping several deities. Maggi was called out for God's purpose. He has use for us all according to Romans 8: "Whom He predestined, these He also called; whom He called, these He also justified; and whom He justified, these He glorified" (Rom. 8:30 NASB). God is!

Maggi wanted to share her experience of kingship with her family. She has worked to bring her parents to the United States as well. I am so elated and joyful over her story of faith. I thank God for her yielding to His call of her unto salvation to help expand His kingdom on earth! We are under the commandment of love, so it is given for us to follow the instructions told us in Matthew 5: "Let our light so shine that men (women) may see our good works and glorify God in Heaven" (Matt. 5:6 KJV).

God's Homework: Mothers are not the only people who perform nurturing acts. Present someone, who is not related to you, with a special token to express his/her value to you.

44

I Would Not Be Denied This Christmas

❧

ERNESTINE MEADOWS MAY

All your children shall be taught by the Lord, and great shall be the peace of your children. (Isa. 54:13 KJV)

Truly I say unto you, unless you turn and become like children, you will never enter the kingdom of heaven (Matt. 18:3 KJV)

This is the story of a little girl who, like most small children, would come to us with trust, excitement, faith, and a belief that all is well. This child had a belief system put into place by paying attention to family norms and the teachings of those involved with her Sunday school church family—beliefs that had started from as early as five years old. It is a trust that has grown and fashioned itself into an anchor that is still a part of her faith-based experiences today. She was a child who was sheltered from the views of the world's way. It became easy for her to believe because it was all that she knew. I think God honored that in her, because He trusted that the gifts of His revelations would be received and shared at a set time in the earth.

There are many facets to God's glory. As I believed, I received the building of my soul by way of experiences, dreams, visions, and visitations. He was at work, developing in me a solid trust in Him. It is so awesome to be reading my journey through journals and rekindle the things He gave me, and now to give to others to share vicariously the wonderment of it all. In all my days, He has always been there with me, which made faith in His Word come alive in me and caused me to lean on Him for trust. I did not question what we should do as Proverbs 3 says, "Trust in the Lord with all thine heart and lean not to your own understanding. In all thy ways acknowledge Him and He shall direct thy path" (Prov. 3:5–6 KJV). This passage is my rest. You've probably already guessed that the little girl is I! Although my family lived below the nation's poverty guidelines on the economic scale, all of our needs were met as it pertained to provisions. I had no inhibitions, fear, or doubts about what I could or could not do.

It was nearing Christmas, one year, and my brothers would not be around to go into the woods to chop down a cedar tree for Momma to decorate. I would imagine she was entertaining a totally different thought train—one that included all of the other things needing to be done. Perhaps she was feeling a sense of relief that now there was only my sister and me to think about. She had, after all, raised a family consisting of her sisters and brothers and a family of seven of our own. It should have been a time for her to relax a little more. But knowing my momma, she lived her life vicariously through providing and making Christmas real for us all. Looking back, I realize it was her favorite time of the year. She would begin baking two to three weeks out from "C" Day. The aromas of apples, oranges, candies, cinnamon, nutmeg, and coconut filled the house daily. She loved sweets.

With all of this going on we had a need for a tree. I supposed I would become the chosen one to make it happen. I went outside to the barn to find the ax that would normally be at the woodpile. There it was. I picked it up without saying a word to anyone about where I was going, not even asking my momma if I could do what I was about to. I did not want to hear a "no" on this one. So off I went. I remember there were woods behind our house, but it was not the way we normally went in search of a tree, wild berries, or pecans. I had already spotted several that could be possibilities the last time we took a ride with my dad, Homer, in the wagon to explore the woods offerings in early fall.

I walked far and deep into the woods not compassing north, south, east, or west, but feeling confident that I could find my way back. I had assumed David's posture, believing Psalm 23: "Even though I walk through the shadow of death, I will fear no evil, for you Lord, are with me; your rod and your staff they comfort me…" (Ps. 23:4 NIV). I was possibly miles from home without a thought of being afraid of who or what stranger I might walk upon. I finally found a medium-sized tree that I could handle on my own. I had noticed how my brothers would chop near the stem of the tree in an angular hacking motion, until the tree no longer had the strength to remain standing on its own and gave away its life forever. Some things were put into the earth for our enjoyment and pleasure. This tree was mine. I dragged the tree home, and we continued our tradition of having a Christmas tree every year—a tradition we carry on even to this day. Never missed.

I often reflect on this experience, as well as others, because they bring back the childish memories that I enjoy today. It is sad that some children do not have the freedom to roam and explore this beautiful earth on their own anymore. I suppose it is a signs of these times. Evil is so prevalent. Opportunities for cruelty and deception are on every corner and even behind our churches. God help us!

We must always keep in mind that God is our ultimate provider. The Bible tells us this in Psalm 84: "For the Lord God is a sun and shield; the Lord bestows favor and honor. No good thing does He withhold from those who walk uprightly" (Ps. 84:11 NRSV).

God's Homework: Write down your favorite holiday experience and draw a picture that represents that experience.

Overcomers by The Word

45

Panic in Tokyo

❧

Gloria Sharpe Smith

I will be with you always, even unto the end of the world.
(Matt. 28:20 CEV)

International exchange and travel for teachers and students can be quite a rewarding experience, as well as being gripped with some unforgettable moments. In 1995, I was teaching in a school system that hosted a group of teachers and students from Osaka, Japan. Upon their arrival in the district, each teacher and student was assigned to a host family that had been carefully screened for compatibility and availability. Both criteria were critical to the exchange program experience. This same procedure also transpired when I and a group of students and fellow teachers traveled to Osaka and Tokyo, Japan.

Many months of planning had taken place before our April departure from Chicago. Our plane was a Boeing 747, also known as a jumbo jet. I was super excited to climb aboard, embarking on the journey with eight students and six other teachers. I was the organizer of the trip and responsible for children whose parents had bestowed their utmost trust in me for their child's safety and well-being. I had already spent many hours in prayer and had solicited prayers from others concerning every detail of the trip. There was not a doubt in my mind that everything would be just fine.

That was exactly the case, until the day panic struck me in the pit of my stomach and dried my mouth. We arrived safely in Tokyo after enjoying various schools, businesses, and tourist spots in Osaka. My host family in Tokyo was a very civic-minded couple. The husband was a top executive in the Tokyo banking industry and his wife, our hostess, was a community activist for the school system. She was very knowledgeable and had a hand in arranging activities and tours for us.

One particular day, my colleague and I were served a tasty, traditional Japanese breakfast which consisted of steamed rice, miso soup, eggs, and vegetables. We enjoyed our fill and departed the house for a city tour that our hostess teacher had prearranged for the group. We were all set to meet with the others at a designated government building in Tokyo. We had our printed itineraries for the day and were excited to tour this renowned city.

Our hostess spoke English well, but neither my colleague nor I spoke Japanese. Thus far, throughout our trip, the language barrier had not been an issue or even a concern. When we stepped outside of the house, there was a taxi with a Japanese driver waiting for us. The hostess gave him instructions to take us to the predetermined meeting place so we could join our group. Off we went. Once we were dropped together at the meeting spot and saw everyone, we all began to get excited. Everyone was ready for a great day.

The streets of Tokyo were congested. Both sides of the roads were lined with tall, modern buildings of glass and steel that glistened in the bright sunlight. I was in awe, even if I couldn't read a single billboard or street sign. As we were riding along comfortably, looking out of the window intently trying to capture every site, it occurred to me that our driver was no longer following the taxies that were transporting the other students and colleagues. Panic set in! Our driver didn't speak English. We couldn't communicate with him to ask why we were no longer following the others! The fear of being lost and separated, without any idea as to where we were or where we were going was overworking my heart! I said to my colleague, "Let's pray." She was just as anxious. We agreed immediately that prayer was needed.

I remember saying urgently, "Lord, you know where we are and where our other group members are. You know where we're supposed to be. We don't know the language, but You do! Please keep us safe and reconnect us with our group. In Jesus' name. Amen."

This simple prayer, along with our faith, worked. We never spoke a word to the driver. We just prayed quietly, encouraging ourselves in God's faithfulness and His promise to always be with us. Our ultimate trust had been placed in Him, not only for *our* safety, but for all of the students and other teachers as well. As far as I was concerned, *everyone* was lost, except God.

After what seemed to be the longest taxi ride of my life, we finally arrived at a tall, impressive-looking building. Standing right in front were all of the familiar, smiling faces that we knew in Tokyo. "Relief! Thank you, Jesus!" I couldn't keep myself from smiling as I uttered those words out loud. My fear and anxiety were gone. I was no longer feeling lost. Everyone else had been found. Feeling nothing but gratitude, my heart was now calm with joy.

It's very comforting to know that God is a promise keeper. The only way you get to know this is through life experiences with Him.

God's Homework: The next time you feel lost, reach out to God first. Ask Him to place the right people or resources in your path.

46

Overcomers by the Word

SHELLEY M. FISHER, PH.D.

I can do all things through Christ who Strengthens me.
(Phil. 4:13 KJV).

Words can edify. They paint beautiful pictures that can soothe, hurt, encourage healing, and make us whole. I try not to emphasize just any words, but the Word of the Lord. God spoke the world into existence. Everything was made with God's anointed Words, which destroy yokes. The Word of the Lord is full of power and effectual like no other words.

In days past, God spoke to man through His prophets. They were His mouthpieces, declaring His Will on the earth. The prophets were a diverse culture that encountered many toils and trouble to render the Lord's Word to His people, who often did not want to hear it.

Today, we have a Bible, written by men inspired by the Holy Spirit, and of which no jot or tittle is to be subtracted or added. The promises contained in the Bible are, yea and amen, our blueprint for living. For every situation we could encounter, there is a Scripture to address the concern. God tells us to meditate on His Word day and night, that we may find good success and make our way prosperous (Josh. 1:8 KJV author's paraphrase).

There are multitudes who profess Christ as their personal Lord and Savior, but who do not have the revelation of the value of His

Word, the covenant promises of Jesus, and the life-giving nature of the Word. The Word is life to those who find it and health to all their flesh.

The book of John, chapter 1 tells us that "In the beginning was the Word and the Word was with God and the Word was God and that all things were made by Him and without Him was not anything made that was made. In Him was light and the light shines in the darkness, and the darkness did not comprehend" (John 1:3 NKJV). The Scripture speaks of John coming to bear witness of the Light, but he was not the light. Jesus, the true light, is highlighted. He came unto His own and His own received Him not, but to as many as received Him, gave He the power to become the sons of God who were born, not of blood, nor of the will of the flesh, nor of the will of man, but of God.

Jesus and His Word are one. The Bible has much to say about the importance of God's Word. Proverbs 4 states, "My son, attend to my words; incline thine ear unto my sayings. Let them not depart from thine eyes; keep them in the midst of thine heart. For they are life unto those that find them, and health to all their flesh" (Prov. 4:20–22 KJV).

David said of the Word, "Lord, your word have I hidden in my heart that I may not sin against You" (Ps. 119:10 NKJV). The Word of the Lord will keep you on the straight and narrow. Your love for the Word will constrain you and cause you to do His will. The Word will create in you such a love for the Lord that you will find it difficult to satiate your desire for Him. There are no other words like the Word of God.

I used to have a love for Shakespeare and Chaucer. I could even quote the long soliloquy by McBeth or Caesar's speech of Brutus's betrayal. Maybe, even stranger, I would read Chaucer in Old English, because I liked the cadence. But when I discovered the Bible, the words of our Lord and Savior and His precepts, I abandoned Shakespeare and Chaucer. I was stuck in Isaiah 6, memorizing it, getting it down into the crevices of my soul. I know now it was a setup by my heavenly Father, beckoning me into ministry.

God's Words are wisdom, knowledge, understanding, and life. A case in point is this Scripture: "Lord order my steps. I will instruct you and teach you in the way which you shall go. I will guide you with mine eye"(Ps. 32:8 NKJV).

Whenever I seem to be at a standstill, I seek the Lord for His guidance. I know to follow the Scripture in John 8: "Continue in my word and you will be my disciple indeed" (John 8:31–32 NKJV).

God's Homework: The Word is medicine to your soul, body, and spirit. Take it in daily and allow it to do the Lord's work for you. The Word is the Balm in Gilead, the sufficiency to get you the victory. Do you have a word bank to combat the wiles of the enemy and to make your way prosperous to have victory and good success? Compile your word bank to combat the enemy.

47

Synergistic Living

❧

ERNESTINE MEADOWS MAY

*Before they call, I will answer; while they are still
speaking, I will hear.* (Isa. 65:24 NIV)

I t is not magic, or luck, when you live in the overflow or when the
sustenance of your actions produces a combined effect greater
than the sum of their parts. When this happens, you need to consider the source. Philippians 4 states it bluntly, "But my God shall
supply all your needs according to His riches in glory by Christ
Jesus" (Phil. 4:19 NLT). His provisions are more than enough.

Both of our daughters were students at Purdue University at
the same time, overlapping by two years. I need not have to tell you
that money was tight. Their dad went to the credit union where
he worked to secure a loan that would help with tuition and other
expenses only to be told that our debt was greater than our combined incomes. Therefore, the loan officer rendered our application
for a loan as unfavorable at that time. He did not understand the
math of the overcomer! Not everyone understands the phenom-
enal works of God, nor do they know about it. It is not a secret. It
is just that it has not yet been revealed to them by the knowledge
of God's promises. It is available to all believers. We were not
unwise spenders, nor frivolous shoppers, never maxed out credit
cards, or took lavish vacations. We didn't live above our means…
well; yes, we did! God's favor was upon our household. Our credit

was always good. We paid our bills on time. We gave our tithes and offerings to the Lord. That is my trust! To quote Brother Morris Curillo, "Don't look at how big your problem is, look at how big your God is."

I remember a time when our daughters wanted extra money to spend and would ask their dad for it. I heard his response to them as, "You think money grows on *me?*" When he was asleep one night, I went into the closet where he kept his wallet, took it and prayed over it that God would give the increase to satisfy our needs *"according to His riches and glory by Christ Jesus."* I prophesied over the wallet that money would be made available to him. "Money answers all things" (Eccl.10:19). His truck broke down with engine problems and he was laid off from work. His friend, Frances, was very prosperous in vehicles and allowed him to drive one of his, until he was able to get the repairs completed. While laid off from work, he was receiving many calls from people who needed their basements remodeled, or a roof put on their house or siding. By word-of-mouth, he was able to attain odd jobs that used his skills gained in earlier years in carpentry, electrical assembly, and plumbing. His brothers had schooled him well, besides the opportunities afforded him to attend school to certify himself in these crafts. His wallet never suffered from lack in that season of drought, nor until this day of our Lord.

How would we know the fulfillment and the embodiment of the Godhead, in all His power and glory, if we never delivered our trust to Him? He invites us to trust Him for our sufficiency as we call on Him to perform His Word in our lives. To rest in His love for total dependency and obedience is a trust at the peak of our faith. I delight in the Holy Spirit's prompting of me to go deeper and reach higher in Christ Jesus who is the "author and finisher" of my faith according to (Hebrews 12:2 KJV).

In this race marks are missed, opportunities are misunderstood, and diversions turn us from our course, but God remains constant.

He says so in Jeremiah 20, as it states, "...His plan is to prosper us and bring us to an expected (successful) end" (Jer. 20:11 KJV).

God's Homework: Make a list of three things that were surrounded by special circumstances that caused things to pan out in your favor.

48

Factoring Fear

❧

ERNESTINE MEADOWS MAY

Before they call, I will answer; And while they are
still speaking, I will hear. (Isa. 65:24 NKJV)

Dreams have made me aware of the darker side of the spirit realm. Many times, it has been no fun to go through the depths of the abyss. You can see an underlying theme within every spiritual awakening, in every experience, that essentially translates to trust.

I was on the list of Satan himself to take my dreams in another direction. I knew it was him because the ethers changed when he appeared to me. He took me by force to show me the place of his abode. His fruits of the spirit were evil, dark, torment, fear, death, destruction, and robbery. He didn't mind me knowing of them. He has no loyalty to his subjects! In his presence I could not speak, could not pray to give him a command or use my God-given authority against him. He had locked my jaws to prevent me from taking any actions. He was to be in total charge. He knew that if I could speak, he would no longer have power against me! I speak with authority! He knows I will be coached by the Holy Spirit. I had the man on the inside of me that he could not reach. My fight had to be waged from within. I called on the name songs of Jesus and sang songs of Jesus and victory in Him. He would not be short of His promise to never leave me nor forsake me! As

I did this, I could feel the loosening of Satan's hold on me to the point of full exoneration. My Lord and Savior Jesus Christ had redeemed me yet again! I remembered that the Lord spoke to me, on another dream encounter, saying, "*I have already preceded you.*"

He is my comfort. He is my peace. In Him will I trust. I have seen Psalm 139: "If I should go up to heaven, thou art there: If I should go down to hell, thou art present…" (Psalm 139:8 NKJV). This is how I can endure the test of my faith.

This dream happened just after I had completed reading a book by Kenneth Hagin, titled, *Demons and How to Deal with Them*. His focus was on using "commands" and our "authority" as believers to subdue the enemy. Satan wanted to discredit what I had read in Brother Hagin's book. He wanted to put fear into my heart. Fear is a stronghold over our lives. It bears out that by our faith we shall overcome by the blood of the Lamb and the witness of our testimonies. Don't be afraid to tell your story of deliverance so that others will know that their struggles can be claimed as victories in Jesus also.

Tests and trials will come to make you stronger, so just pass the test! Trust God! Believe in Jeremiah 1, which tells us, "And they shall fight against thee; but shall not prevail against thee; for I am with thee, saith the Lord, to deliver thee" (Jer. 1:19 NIV).

God's Homework: Stand and face the nearest mirror. Make the three following affirmations to yourself aloud:

1. I am fearfully and wonderfully made. (Psalm 139:14 NIV)
2. I have not been given a spirit of fear, but I have been given love, power and a sound mind. (2 Tim. 1:17 KJV)
3. With my God, I am able to run through a troop and leap over walls. (Ps. 18:19 AMP)

49

On My Way to Death

ERNESTINE MEADOWS MAY

Whoever dwells in the shelter of the Most High will rest in the shadow of the Almighty. I will say of the Lord, He is my refuge and my fortress, my God, in whom I trust. (Ps. 91:1–2 NIV)

I was really on my way to purchase roller skates from a skate shop I had heard about in Illinois. Nearing an exit, still on the Indiana side, I glanced in my rearview mirror to see a semi-tractor truck proceed to move into my lane. I could tell there was not enough clearance space for him to execute this move. I began blowing my horn loudly and continuously. It was as if he couldn't hear me or see what he was about to do. I had no shoulder to pull on to. It all happened so very fast.

Coming into my lane, so fast and furious, the cab of his truck hit the front driver's side of my car's bumper and threw me into a tailspin that thrust me into the center lane, then off the roadside to a downhill embankment. As I was still rolling downhill, I had a vision flash before my eyes. It was the *Post Tribune* newspaper with the picture of my car wrapped around the telephone pole that I was heading directly into. I had lost control of the vehicle. I had no power to steer and guide myself to a safe place. The newspaper showed the car at its center point— crushed and entangled with the front end kissing the back end of the car—all wrapped and crunched without a sign of life left in it. The headlines on the paper read: "A FATALITY! No Survivors!" But then, God said, *"Not so!"*

The photo was the size of about one fourth of the front page. I'd met death, but faith jumped in between! Faith changed the news that day. God sent His angels to cause me to be a news changer! We can be transformers in life by our belief in Jesus Christ. He is for us, and with us always, even to the end of the world

When the sheriff came, he said the drivers of these trucks sometimes don't get enough sleep. They become incoherent, exhibit poor judgment, and are unable to comprehend logical situations. The driver never stopped. It was as though nothing was visible of the impact that he made on me and my automobile. He sat high and my car was low. I can believe that it was not proposed to happen the way it did. Forget the skates. I was glad to be able to go back home and escape death! But God reassured me, just as He can do for you. Psalms 91 says, "He is my refuge, my fortress, in Him will I trust" (Ps. 91:2 NIV).

God's Homework: Go into your quiet place and say this short prayer:

"Lord, I thank you for every bad situation that you kept me from and any type of disaster. I know You were working on my behalf even when I was not aware of it. Amen"

50

Melody Finds the Lump

SHELLEY M. FISHER, PH.D.

I am *the Lord who heals you.*
(Ex. 15:26 NKJV).

We are friends with a couple and our children are similar ages. Their daughter, Melody, and my daughter, Carolyn, had a penchant for the sciences, but both enjoyed art more. These mutual passions ultimately overrode the possibility of their venturing into science careers after college. Melody was dabbling in make-up and fashion, hoping to open her own boutique one day. Carolyn was still searching by working jobs at high-end fashion stores.

Melody's mother called me one day. The tone in her voice indicated all was not well. She sadly told me that, while taking a shower, Melody had discovered a lump in her breast. We had a group of five ladies who met regularly to pray. We decided that we would ask Melody to join us. But Melody was not having any part of it. We realized she was not "there" yet. However, we continued to pray for her.

Trinity, Melody's mom, was concerned that Melody's gynecologist could not see her for another month. I asked Trinity to retrieve Melody's insurance card so we could call other gynecologists in the area, telling them of the urgency. Trinity found a gynecologist who said she would call Melody at work, if that were permissible, to see if she could come into the office the next day.

Melody was accompanied by her mom the next day. The new doctor sent her for a mammogram. Melody was told they would call the same day with the results of the tests. When the call came through, Melody was in the basement, alone on the computer. The physician confirmed that the lump was cancerous. Melody was supposed to return to her gynecologist the following day.

Melody's parents heard her crying and ran to see what was happening. Both parents began consoling Melody. Trinity began to quote the Word. She asked the Lord to send His Word to heal Melody. She prayed for God to uproot cancer at the core. She covered Melody with the blood of Jesus. Trinity asked for the Lord to control and order their steps and to make Melody whole.

The next day, the doctor's sister saw Melody. She was the head of an oncology department in a major nearby city. They were able to orchestrate, expedite, and get procedures in place in record timing. After the examination, the doctor said she wanted to operate. It was up to Melody to decide if she wanted to keep her breast. Melody opted to only have the lump removed. The doctor said they would keep a close watch on the lymph nodes in the area, especially since Melody's family history indicated traces of cancer.

I went often with Melody and Trinity for the chemotherapy treatments. Melody exhibited a variety of emotions. On the day that the nurse gave us a tour of the chemo room, which was a drab gray and without windows, a loud wail and a swell of tears erupted from Melody, as if a dam had just broken. Trinity and I prayed for another setting for the chemotherapy. The room was narrow and seemed prison-cell-like. God granted the request with a brightly colored room, large reclining chairs and windows with the sunlight dancing throughout. It gave the room a lively jolt. It was a welcome perk that charged the atmosphere positively.

Melody had a team working with her: oncologist, surgeon, psychologist, and nutritionist. On occasion, things would become tense in the waiting room as a young person would start to cry profusely; then a psychologist would emerge. We tried to focus

Melody's attention elsewhere. All the while, Melody had Scriptures concerning her healing that she would recite during the process. After chemotherapy, there were good days and bad days. During the bad, Melody would "sleep it off" more or less. Her spirits remained high while around us. She would tell us what the nutritionist discussed with her, and sometimes she would share what the psychologists said, especially if it included visualizing calm water or sunny places.

Carolyn arranged her schedule to visit with Melody in the evenings after she'd had chemotherapy. Carolyn wanted to be available for her friend and encourage her during her trial. Their friendship thrived during this time. Carolyn was helpful with the loss-of-hair crisis. Melody had long, thick, darkish-brown hair, strikingly pretty tresses. When she awoke in the mornings, clumps of hair would be strewn across her pillow. Carolyn encouraged Melody to cut it all off. Carolyn cut her hair as well; both became "fashionably bald."

The radiation therapy did not seem to be as intense. We had to remain in the waiting room. Most days Melody would return in smiles.

At that time, a fairly new drug, Tamoxifen, was being used for a period of five years after completing treatment, to reduce the chances of breast cancer returning in high-risk patients. Melody kept a positive attitude and meditated on her Scriptures for healing. Her parents and the prayer group continued in prayer throughout the process for the entire year-and-a-half of treatments of chemotherapy, radiation, and Herceptin.

Melody adjusted well, returned to her artsy ventures for a while, then went to work for a technology company with emphasis on fashion design. Today, she continues to live a healthy lifestyle—diet, exercise, no medications, except for her spiritual diet of Scriptures.

Fourteen years later, Melody remains healthy, whole, and happy. God is a healer and can do exceedingly abundantly above all that you can think or ask. He wants us to cast our cares on Him and to position ourselves to receive. "God is no respecter of persons" (Acts 10:34 KJV). He healed Melody, and we can receive healing from Him also. Nothing is too difficult for God.

Trials come to make us strong. Within circumstances there are opportunities for growth, learning, and entering into a deeper relationship with God. He has our destinies in His hands. If we cooperate with Him, He will reveal purpose and destiny to us.

We should surround ourselves with positive people who know the Word of God and demonstrate faith in Him. God will instruct us and teach us during the times when ill winds are blowing in our lives. God will bring us through to winds of change and victory.

Cancer is a mere word to God. He has conquered death and all diseases with the thirty-three stripes that he took across His back while He was flogged on the way to the cross. Get the Word on the inside of you as Ezekiel did. Eat the scroll (the Word) and when adverse situations arise in your life you can say it is written: "But Lord, you will restore me to health and heal my wounds,' declares the Lord" (Jer. 30:17 NKJV). Recite Scripture verses, such as, "You restore me to health and let me live..." (Isa 38:16–17 NKJV). Know that your Father has called you beloved. "Beloved, I wish above all things that you may prosper and be in good health even as your soul prospers" (3 John 2 NKJV).

You do not have to be overwhelmed with health problems; the Word of God can be your supernatural help. Seek and you shall find. Knock and it shall be opened to you. (Matt. 7:7 NKJV). Your heavenly Father knows what you need before you ask. He is beckoning you now to come unto him for His yoke is easy and His burden is light, and you will find rest for your soul.

What is your need? Ask Him. He awaits your request. He loves you so much that He laid down His life for you that you might be whole and free in the here and now. He is knocking. Won't you hear and answer his call? Won't you allow Him in to reveal Himself to you as Healer? Romans 10 asserts, "If you will believe in your heart and confess with your mouth that Jesus Christ is

Lord you shall be saved. For with the heart one believes unto righteousness, and with the mouth confession is made unto salvation" (Rom. 10:9–10 NKJV). Say this aloud and allow the Lord into your heart. He will do for you things that you have never imagined and take you places you have never been. "For I will restore health to you, and I will heal you of your wounds, says the Lord" (Jer. 30:17 NKJV). God is stirring the waters. Will you be made whole?

God's Homework: Diseases are nothing but a word to God because on the cross He overcame all diseases. Are you relying on Him and keeping your faith operative during challenging times by speaking the Word?

Speak the Word over yourself: "God, You sent Your Word and healed me" (Psalm 107:20).

51

Elephant's Eye Lashes

SHELLEY M. FISHER, PH.D.

Surely, He shall deliver you from the snare of the fowler and from the perilous pestilence. (Psalm 91:3 NKJV)

Johannesburg, Soweto, Sun City, Durbin—yes, South Africa! My husband, daughter, and I were excited to visit. It was a dream come true. There were such contrasts in the places we visited—from shanty towns to visiting royalty and having high tea. Our tour sponsor had lived in South Africa during Apartheid for many years, before relocating home again to Washington D.C. We had insights as to where to go.

We visited schools and an orphanage. The children at the orphanage held on to my daughter and did not want to let her leave. Restaurants, royalty, marketplaces, and watching the sunrise on the Indian Ocean were enjoyable, but not as exciting as the safari.

After breakfast, our group prepared for the event. I had seen safaris in movies and was anticipating our trip. In the area, wild animals just roamed. We were told not to leave our vehicles. Our group was in a tram with the windows open because of the heat. My daughter and I sat on seats behind each other. My husband sat near the front talking to the driver, Diamini. As we passed through the grounds, we saw people defying the rules by stepping outside of their cars and taking pictures. We saw a hyena trying to enter a car window. These were the most beautiful animals I had ever seen—lions, zebras, rhinos, giraffes—God's creatures. We were also taking pictures. We wanted to savor the beauty of the animals when we returned to America. There was laughing and chatter throughout the tram.

At times, the vehicles would crowd together and other times the traffic would become sparse for a while. In one congested spot, Diamini told us to look at the animals ahead. There was a herd of elephants, some with babies standing in front of their parents. Then it happened. One of the vehicles passed through a space between a baby elephant and its mother. Instantly, the elephants encircled the vehicles. They seemed to be coming from everywhere. They began to make shrill loud cries. Diamini explained it was a war cry. My daughter jumped in the seat with the man across the aisle, because the elephants were walking up to our side of the tram. Most of the other people were moving away from the windows. I was about to move when I saw the elephant's eyelashes. I stopped in my tracks thinking, "*Look at those eyelashes. They must be five inches long!*" Here I was, in imminent danger, yet mesmerized by the elephant's eyelashes. I finally broke away and moved.

While in motion, I said a one-line-prayer, "Lord, help us get out of here safely."

The war cry grew louder and louder. My husband was talking to Diamini. I kept wondering what they could possibly be talking about at a time like this. Suddenly, there was a loud throttling sound and we jerked forward. Diamini gunned the motor, and we went through a small opening between the elephants. Diamini laughed, saying the elephants wanted to have us for dinner. No one else laughed. It began to rain. We pulled over while the men put the windows up. The atmosphere was sober as we rode in silence for forty-five minutes back to the hotel.

After arriving at the hotel, Diamini opened the doors and greeted us as we exited. Suddenly everyone was laughing and imitating Diamini's accent.

"The elephants wanted to have us for dinner."

I noticed all of the men placing something in Diamini's hand. It was a tip, as if to say, thank you! "But those who hope in the LORD will renew their strength. They will soar on wings like eagles; they will run and not grow weary, they will walk and not be faint" (Isa, 40:31 NKJV).

The Word says, "I will give angels charge over you to keep you in all your ways…" (Ps. 91:11). I would say, even when you are mesmerized by an elephant's five-inch eyelashes, God is still your protector.

God's Homework: You may get in a predicament that is not of your choosing. But God is waiting to come to your rescue when you call upon Him. He has a way out. Do you remember that God will never leave you nor forsake you in tenuous times? Give God first place in your heart. He is always with you. Call upon Him.

52

A Mona Miracle

ERNESTINE MEADOWS MAY

Peace I leave with you; my peace I give to you. Not as the world gives do I give to you. Let not your hearts be troubled, neither let them be afraid. (John 14:27 ESV)

Approaching my front door, after returning home from the kids' dental appointment, I had rushed into the house upon hearing the telephone ringing. Mona, who was four years old at the time, had hollered across the street to her friends, Christy, Che and Greg who were outside playing in their yard. I didn't think much of it because I was rushing to catch the phone before the last ring. I picked up the phone and had just gotten past the hello part when I heard the loud screeching of a fast-driven vehicle, followed by a crashing "BOOM." I threw the phone down. I could only think of my little baby being vulnerable to the catastrophe that I was hearing.

As I ran out of the house, I saw Mona jumping up from the ground, looking startled and incoherent, snapping her head in the direction of her friend, Christy's house. She walked away from the vehicle to continue across the street. I quickly followed to pick her up and try to understand what had just happened. The driver of the automobile was out of his car looking puzzled, relieved, and frightened—all at the same time. He had just rounded the curve at the corner of the block at full speed, applied his brakes too late and made contact with my child. The average weight of a car would have been from 2,900 to 3,500 pounds— against her tiny frame of about forty-eight-pounds . That, ladies and gentlemen, is called a miracle, and it happened on Rush Street!

The driver and I exchanged information as one of our neighbors called paramedics. Mona was rushed to the hospital for a thorough check and found to be awesomely well! She was actually released to come home at the same hour. Do not doubt that miracles are happening in the world today. I have witnessed a few in my lifetime. I could not believe, nor could I understand the quiet peace that quieted my entire being. This one is very near and dear to me. Remember to heed Proverbs 3: "Trust in the Lord with all your heart; and lean not to your own understanding. In all your ways acknowledge him, and he shall direct your paths" (Proverb 3:5–6 NIV).

God's Homework: The next time you see a child, stop and whisper a prayer to God on behalf of all children and ask Him to bless them!

53

Overcoming Fear

❧

ERNESTINE MEADOWS MAY

For the weapons of our warfare are not carnal but mighty through
God to the pulling down of strongholds. (Proverb 3:5–6 NIV)

As I've said many times before, God has given me a glimpse into the supernatural world. It is a world where satanic spirits dwell. Their renderings are to make us helpless, fearful, and powerless. These spirits intend to destroy our will to stay on the course that God has set for each of us. Demonic presence is intimidating and overwhelming to the natural man. However, we are of spirit, body, and soul. These three operate like the gears that shift in an automobile. Each requires a mindset of overcoming, of power, and of victory while clothed in an emphatically specialized uniform.

I believe fear is the greatest weapon Satan uses against us. It festers in our mind, attacking us in our souls, causing our emotions to overreact. Once this state has occurred, it then becomes our decision to embody these emotions or change our way of thinking. The Bible tells us in Proverbs 23: "As a man thinks in his heart, so is he" (Proverb 23:7 KJV). What we think precedes what we react to. In all things, I refuse to stagger at the promises of God. When we practice faith on a daily basis, it becomes our default lifeline.

Isaiah 41 tells us to "Fear not, for I am with you; be not dismayed, for I am your God. I will strengthen you, Yes, I will help you, I will uphold you with my righteous right hand" (Isaiah 41:10

KJV). Fear also creates stumbling blocks to our spiritual growth and development.

I am reminded of a time when a mysterious manifestation of satanic works happened to discourage a group of sisters from joining God First Ministries under the leadership of Dr. Mildred C. Harris, of Chicago, Illinois. On this particular evening, a group of women from Gary traveled to Chicago for the induction ceremony for new members. It was with happy hearts and clear skies that we journeyed together in one car. Suddenly, about halfway from the Illinois border, near the toll booth, the atmosphere began to change. Dark clouds rolled up from nowhere. Intense thunder and lightning erupted suddenly. Rain with intermittent hail pelted the car to the point of almost zero visibility.

I was the designated driver. I observed many cars pulling to the side of the tollway to wait out this tumultuous creation of a demonic kind. Trees were swaying from both sides of the tollway easements, forming a canopy for our dark passage through the tunnel. It was darker than dark. It looked like a day of doom. None of us could help but wonder, *Was the world coming to an end at this moment? Were we ready for the rapture?* Satan wanted us to become discouraged —and afraid. He wanted us to turn around and go home. I decided to press forward as I heard one sister reading from the Book of Psalms. Someone else was praying and I heard sweet songs of deliverance. We were all on one accord to the glory of God! That self same power that Jesus spoke to calm the storm, as he vocalized, *"Peace be Still,"* in Mark 4:39 (KJV), was also in us. It was a setup on both sides. The enemy tried to thwart our plans, but God had a greater plan of overcoming and canceling what the enemy meant for evil. God turned it to our good. He intends for us to confront what comes our way, as David did in Psalm 91: "I will not be afraid of the terror at night, nor for the arrow that flieth by day" (Ps. 91:5 KJV).

We began to see slivers of sun peeking through the clouds. They gradually moved aside to expose the same clear blue sky that we had begun our journey with. The rain had almost stopped, except for a few droplets left to be squeezed out of the clouds to barely a drizzle. Looking to the sides of the tollway, as we drove the earth, there was no evidence of rainwater to be seen. We looked at each other with overwhelming disbelief. We each knew that it was a spiritual battle orchestrated by the enemy but fought by God on our behalf. God delivers! Yet, He wanted us to experience the real tactics of the enemy and the ensuing deliverance offered us when we trust Him.

When we met with the ladies at the God First Headquarters, we asked them about their weather conditions, as compared to our experience. There were none to compare. On any given day one can travel the same route we took to Chicago from Gary, Indiana. You will not see a line of trees on either side of the tollway that could form the canopy that we traveled beneath on that evening. You'll probably not experience the depth of darkness, nor the pelting of elements that had to be included in order for Satan to get to us. We must fight carnal with carnal and spiritual warfare with spiritual weapons. The enemy tried to stop us from receiving what God had in store for us for this ministry. We received a power-packed Word and a prophetic impartation as our reward of faith. I invite you, our precious readers, to receive this wonderful witness that you may grow in faith and in the power of our Creator.

God's Homework: Is there a service you can render from your area of expertise or a passion you have that could be beneficial to a group or organization? Make a list of groups you would be interested in joining.

54

Baby Prayers

❦

GLORIA SHARPE SMITH

*And God blessed them, and God said unto them, Be fruitful, and
multiply, and replenish the earth, and subdue it.*
(Gen. 1:28a KJV)

I t doesn't matter if I am in a church service, at a conference,
a women's retreat, or facilitating a workshop, inevitably I will
get called upon to join other intercessors to pray for individuals
who desire prayer. And, interestingly, several people will have the
same requests. Most often, they are centered around employment,
financial needs, or health issues. And I certainly get my share
of requests to pray for marriages and wayward children. There
are even requests for loved ones to be saved or to come into the
saving knowledge of Jesus Christ. All of these remain very standard requests. The most memorable ones are those that are made
by couples who desire to have children and are having difficulty
conceiving. Most have been told by a physician that it just isn't
going to happen. The medical field cannot seem to offer any hope
to these couples who are desiring so desperately to "be fruitful
and multiply."

I always feel when these couples ask for prayer, that their faith
is being put on display and that my faith will be strengthened by
praying for them. It is time for faith to go to work! I can exercise
my own faith and trust God to honor His word, by rewarding

them openly with a beautiful child, a living witness. I just always choose to believe that God will honor the desires of their hearts and that He has me there just for them.

My first prayer request regarding conception was from a young couple who had been married for several years. Both husband and wife had gone through all of the traditional testing. The final word was that the husband had a very low sperm count, only two (to be exact). According to the doctor, this was the, seemingly, impossible mountain that could not be moved. Well, we prayed and believed differently. I reminded the young man that he had two sperm and that it only took one to get the job done. He was in agreement.

"Just do what you need to do, and God will do the rest," I told him with confidence.

Months later, my phone rang and the person on the other end of the line was his wife. I heard her familiar voice, using my nickname, "NuNu?" There was something in the tone of her voice that prompted me to immediately say, "You're pregnant!"

With joy she responded, "How did you know?"

I replied that the Spirit of the Lord had just told me. We rejoiced together that our prayers had been answered. The couple experienced a perfect, full-term pregnancy, along with the normal delivery of a beautiful, healthy, baby girl. God continued to answer their prayers and blessed them with two more children.

The outcome of my first experience made it easy for me to pray in agreement with another young couple that approached me. Their triple prayer requests were very specific:

They wanted to have children and had not been successful.

They wanted to move to another area.

The husband was seeking employment.

I prayed with them, assuring them that God was able to answer all three concerns. Of course, I told them about the couple that I had prayed for and how God had blessed them with three children, and added that I would be seeking Him to do the same for them. I wanted to encourage them in their faith and give them hope. I was counting on God to be faithful again. I also thought that fate had brought this couple specifically to me because of my prior experience.

Sometime later, at church, the young couple approached me and my husband. They admitted that they had been observing us on Sundays and requested that we mentor them. We were honored and excited about the potential of such a special relationship. During this time, my husband and I were group leaders for our church. We hosted meetings twice a month in our home. Although this couple did not live in our area, I invited them to join us for a meeting and they did. It was an excellent fit. They continued attendance and through these interactions, we began to witness prayers being answered. First, the husband got a new job; then they moved to an area that was much closer to us. It was ideal. Two prayers had been answered and there was one more to go.

From time to time, I would jokingly ask, "How are things going?"

Sammy, the husband, would smile bashfully and say, "Oh, I don't know."

I could tell that the waiting was weighing heavily on his wife. She was not handling the monthly disappointment very well.

One evening as they were leaving, I said, "Sammy we're still trusting God; you just stay busy and do what you're supposed to do and leave the rest up to the Lord."

We had a big laugh that seemed to ease the pain and lighten the mood.

A few weeks later, I learned that one of the group members had been diagnosed with breast cancer. I was led by the Spirit to anoint her in oil and pray for her. After I finished, the Spirit spoke to me and said, *"Anoint Sandra's belly with oil and pray for her."* I explained my instructions to Sandra. She stood there with a big smile on her face and gladly pulled her top up to expose the part of her body that she longed to be filled with a gift from God. As I spread the oil, I kept thinking about a verse from the Bible.

"Children are a gift from the LORD; they are a reward from him" (Ps. 127:3 NLT).

More waiting. A few more months passed before there was a real sign that something might be happening. I noticed Sandra, sitting on the sofa, leaning back with her head somewhat bowed. She appeared to be uncomfortable. Her countenance was sad.

I spoke up and said, "Sandra, are you okay?"

She said, "I'm not feeling too well."

I replied, "Maybe something is going on."

She responded, "No, I don't think so."

Then her husband, who was standing close by said, "You know, she's not been feeling well for the last few days."

And I replied with, "Sandra, don't say no! We're praying in agreement for something to happen! Keep praying and believing and don't speak against what we are praying for."

She flashed a smile, chuckled and said, "All right."

Her husband told me that she had a doctor's appointment scheduled for later the next week. Our meeting was over. It would be another two weeks before I would see them again. But the following Tuesday, my cell phone rang. Once again, I heard "NuNu," this time from Sandra's soft voice. She was still at the doctor's office. We both experienced unspeakable joy because there was evidence that our prayers had been answered. She went on to give birth to a beautiful baby girl. My husband and I were honored when we were asked to be her godparents. It was such a blessing to be a part of this family's life and to share in their story of God's faithfulness.

I never had any doubt that the Lord would not bless them with a child. It was the doctor that had not given Sandra any hope. She was totally amazed and has since had the opportunity to deliver two more girls. It's interesting to note here, that after many months of disappointment, Sandra says she remembers riding home from church one Sunday and thinking, *"Lord, just one. Just one, please!"* He not only gave her one, but decided to triple her blessings!

These experiences prepared me for what was to come later when I was invited to facilitate prayer at a women's retreat. It was customary for me to lead a faith walk and pray with the young women on Saturday morning. And this particular year there were a number of women who requested prayer because they wanted a child, that special gift from God. Of course, I thought of my other victories in this area and knew that "Baby Blessings" were on the way. Because of God's faithfulness and His word, my faith was not challenged. I was there for them. However, what occurred surpassed anything that I could have imagined. Years later, I heard from one of the ladies who had been a member of the church that had sponsored the retreat. She was on the prayer team with me while in preparation for the retreat and during our time there. She shared that during a span of four years, there had been thirty-one births! They were all related to the prayers that we had prayed for the women who had attended the retreat. God had been steadily multiplying and performing his Word.

Prayers don't always get answered as immediately as we would like, but they *do* get answered. We can trust in Him that the results will always be in our best interest. His timing and ways are perfect. If you have a request that you have placed before the Lord, you can take this Scripture to heart and wait on him:

> For truly, I say to you, if you have faith like a grain of mustard seed, you will say to this mountain, "Move from here to there," and it will move, and nothing will be impossible for you. (Matt. 17:20b ESV)

You will eventually, but absolutely, be pleased with the end result. Each test or challenge that we face, and then experience success, prepares us for the next one. My prayer for you is that your faith will be multiplied.

God's Homework: Dare to pray and believe for God to answer something that seems impossible (to you) in His own time. Also— ask another individual to agree with you in this prayer.

55

Prayer

⌘

Shelley M. Fisher, Ph.D.

Men always ought to pray and not lose heart.
(Luke 18:1 NKJV)

I've talked about intercessory prayer as standing in the gap and making up the hedge for the land, standing in place of others. I am a prophetic intercessor, one who hears the voice of God, and prays His will. However, it was not always this way.

I remember when someone at church would ask me to pray on a special occasion and I would ask my husband to write me a prayer. His response was, in essence, "I do not know what is in your heart."

And my reply was, "Just write the prayer, please."

I have come to know what he meant by not knowing what is in your heart. When you love God, you want what He wants. His desires are in your heart.

During the time that I was in the educator's group, I learned to pray. The mentor of the group placed a lot of emphasis on prayer. This was a time when I was so hungry for the Word that I devoured it. I'd been a voracious reader, prior to this, and my passion for reading was transferred to the Bible. I learned the meaning of the Paraclete, the Teacher, or the Holy Spirit.

What was happening to me was new. I'd attended our prayer meetings at church. When I prayed, it was if the Paraclete came right alongside me. I could feel the presence of the Holy Spirit speaking and moving through me. I just opened my mouth and Scripture rolled out of my mouth with fervency. It seemed that *I* was not there at all—only the Holy Spirit, praying with fire and fervency. I knew it was not me.

My then pastor would make remarks such as, "If I had a match, I would set you on fire."

I was not sure what he meant, but I knew it was disparaging. In subsequent meetings, I would try not to pray, but before I knew it, I was on my feet. I could imagine what Jeremiah meant when he said the Word was like fire shut up in his bones.

When believers study and focus on the Word, the Holy Spirit will pray through them. Praying the Word is the way I was taught to pray. God's Word is anointed and full of power.

Within spiritual groups, I was the rookie Christian. At times, the seasoned Christians seemed to disapprove of the way I prayed. I never understood that, but I think you should pray the way God tells you to pray. When your focus is on Him, you do not have time to dissect or critique someone else's prayer because they do not pray the way you do. There should not be any competition in the arena of prayer.

In retrospect, I can see that God used me to impact the prayer group at church. Noticeably, people started to quote Scriptures and to abandon King James English while praying. God has an assignment for each of us. We do not dictate the assignment but yield to His leading.

Praying the Word allows us to experience God's presence.

Prayer is the way to God. It is through prayer that we enter into a relationship with our Lord and Savior. We learn to hear His voice, obey, and do His bidding on the earth. "God is a spirit and they who worship Him must worship Him in spirit and in truth" (John 4:24 NKJV).

A cautionary note: The Bible tells us that God will not hear our prayers if we have unforgiveness in our hearts. There are times when we must ask the Holy Spirit to search us and to let us know if anything within us is not of God. We always want to position ourselves to hear from God.

God's Homework: Are you keeping the fervency and fire in your prayer life? Your relationship with God, time spent in prayer and in His presence, will stoke the flames of fire to pray. There is an urgency to pray and to touch lives. As you pray for others, God will perform a work in you. Pray!

56

Give Me a Drink

SHELLEY M. FISHER, PH.D.

Ho! Everyone who thirsts, Come to the waters...
(Isa. 55:1 NKJV)

Often, as I read my Bible, I am inspired to go to a particular book. On this day, I was led to John 8, with emphasis on the lady at the well. Remember the story where Jesus and his disciples went their separate ways? Jesus had insisted He had to go to Samaria. As he is at the well, a woman unknown to Him approaches. He tells her personal things about herself. He reveals that He knows the man she currently lives with is not her husband. She perceived He was a prophet.

Then, Jesus tells her that He wants to give her water so that she would never thirst again. She responds practically by pointing out that He doesn't have anything with which to draw water. Jesus asks that she give Him a drink.

After reading the passage, I felt as though the Lord was speaking to me and asking me to give Him a drink, and I thought, *"But Lord, You are the Living Water, the Fountain of Life. I come to You, the Fount, to be filled."*

But I heard the voice again. I sensed the Lord saying to me, *"Give of yourself to me, empty yourself; give me a drink. Give up the old Shelley, that is in you that I cannot use to build my kingdom. Give up all of yourself to Me, so that I can use you to get My will done on the earth. Let me fill you with more of Myself. Empty yourself."*

The Lord will guide, lead, and instruct us in wisdom if we allow it. His ways are not our ways and those who worship Him must worship Him in spirit and in truth. He made us hear and to obey His voice. He purges us because we have been in the world and His kingdom is not of the world. In the scenario with the woman at the well, Jewish society condemned Jews for associating with Samaritans, but Our Lord and Savior insisted on going there. He had a plan for the woman at the well. In fact, she is cited as being the first female evangelist. She ran through the town telling people to come and see a man who told her all about herself. She was evangelizing!

At other times, John 8:31 has been solace for me. When I do not seem to hear from the Lord, although I know He is always speaking, I meditate on this verse. "If you continue in my word (abide), you are my disciples indeed." Jesus has a plan for our lives and strategically orchestrates these plans through both people and various situations. God does not intend for us to be perplexed, disillusioned, or in despair. He knows where we are in Him. I like to say He gives equal opportunities.

In the academic classroom, if you fail or miss the test, you may not get to do a make-up. However, with Jesus, you can take the test over and over, as many times as needed, until you pass it. Hearing and obeying His voice must be developed by reading and meditating His Word, sitting quietly in His presence, fellowshipping with others who know Him and developing a consistent prayer life. Give Him a drink.

God's Homework: Becoming sensitive to God's voice is needed for maturity in your Christian walk. Jesus is always speaking. Do you hear Him? Read your Word and spend time in His presence to get to know His voice. He is a guide who will always lead you in the right direction.

57

Trust God in Unprecedented Moves During Pandemic Times

<figure>ornament</figure>

ERNESTINE MEADOWS MAY

He said to his disciples, 'Why are you so afraid? Do
you still have no faith? (Mark 4:40 NIV)

O ur generation and beyond will always remember the year
2020, because it became a time of unprecedented moves and
changes, globally. Each individual now has a different story and a
different interpretation of what went on. I see it through the lens
of natural eyes, but I have a switchover lens that sees it from the
spiritual perspective. Keep in mind that everyone sees differently,
no matter that we all experience some of the same fallout.

In spite of a hazmat mask, sanitizer, disinfectant, handwashing
ceremonies, or social distancing, medical knowledge could not save
millions of people who tested positive for the coronavirus in just
a few months. Adjustments had to be made to our lifestyles. The
greatest opportunity I see in this is the reckoning of change—the
summons to godly relationships, the invitation to come to repentance and the favorable time for change. There is no going back
to life as it once was. The shutdown can be viewed as a sign of a
new season dawning on the horizon.

During this time of being and of His ideal grace, I've found a story to tell. It is a story to reveal to the world that God cares about the little things that He promotes in and through us. I, like many others, had my plans in place to go back to Chicago and help my Spiritual Mother plan and execute a God-given mandate for an International Prayer Breakfast. It was a huge undertaking to do the will of the Lord for the city, as well as globally. I had received many godly teachings and principles under her ministry and leadership. It was time for me to execute in an outward action that had been deposited in me for the past years of my life. I decided I needed to make a change for better spiritual efficiency of my faith in God. I needed to come up to a higher level of expectation in Him. Dealing with your flesh is, most times, hidden from self. You think of yourself as good because of the annoyance of pride. Ask God to reveal your shortcomings and then pray that He will give you a teachable spirit to receive from His Holy Spirit.

Our home was sold just as the pandemic swept through the world. Our daughter, Mona, had been blessed to receive her real estate license and she listed it on the seller's market. Remarkably it had sold within ten days of the listing. We were caught in the crosshairs of Covid-19, which prevented us from house hunting. I was anticipating what God was up to. No one could possibly predict how long this devastation would last. It was a beast of another kind! The economy slowed to a paltry tailspin, which meant that the city did not have inspectors available to do home permits for remodeling. Our daughter, Kelly's, basement level of her home would have provided housing until a time when searching for a new home would be more feasible. That meant we would probably have a pretty lengthy waiting period.

I had never lived in the city, never lived in an apartment, and the idea of me making such a move appealed to me. It was a time I could use to complete the book I had put aside because of what they call, "writer's block." My personal affirmation was to do just that. I also had been asked to transcribe into text another book for my cousin, Charles, who wanted to write his memoirs. My time could be well spent for the balance of the year. I was committed to this execution.

While I had a plan in place, guess what? God had a greater one that I would also default to:

- A time to reflect and rehearse the deeds of the Lord in my life and for those to come.
* God is now making this possible for me in these pandemic times assuring me that there's more to come. Life goes on. He is with me always, as He has promised.
* Rest in Him (the highest form of trust) and cast all of my cares on Him for He cares!
* Declare and decree, establish the Word of God in heart and in the land as He would have it. Let His word be true.
* When you hear or see the negative spoken, put a trail of a tail at the end of the action using a transitional word to negate the negative with a positive ending. Nevertheless!

I found an apartment building that appealed to me. I wanted to be sure it was the one, as I continued to search for others to compare it with. "Number 77" was significant in its address. I kept coming back to it. The photos were very attractive. I could see myself there. I made an appointment to visit a high-rise that claimed to be a "luxury" residence in the heart of midtown Atlanta. It was better than sufficient for me. I had never lived in an apartment and wanted to experience this type of lifestyle. I was all set for a one-year retreat and the desire of my heart many years ago would now be realized in that God had reserved the right to honor me at this time. I moved in.

A revelation of genuineness of purpose began to come to light for me. I needed to begin this next season of my life knowing God in a way that I had not known Him before. I needed a download of His plan for this latter day. I was ready for His teaching. I needed Him more than I've ever needed Him. I needed to make Him known to whomever had a listening ear to what would be withdrawn from my deposits.

From my balcony I began to visually see the need for prayer through the people on the street. There was a homeless man creating a space under the roof of a closed business. I could see the world from a vantage point of masses and dwelling places, representing the nations of the world. I wanted a newly created me to deal with the post pandemic changes that we would experience by our faith in Jesus Christ, our Victor!

One day, while eating near the doorway of my balcony, I watched a homeless man and gave attention to a thought that came to mind. I began to hear this voice within me, in essence, asking me how I could live in comfort, eating, drinking, and sleeping without any cares when my brother is without? A call of my spirit to have me know that I had a mission to accomplish was right here under my nose. I knew what that meant. I was like Esther, "and who knoweth whether thou art come . . . for such a time as this'" (Esther 4:14 KJV).

The weather was beginning to be cooler in the evenings. I would see my friend huddled under the awning of the building across the street. I remembered my daughter, Kelly, called the family together two Christmases ago to make blankets for the homeless in our community. We did not get to distribute everything. I found some of the blankets. Kelly contributed a backpack with personal essentials. I included one of the blankets that I had made that year. The next night, after I delivered the pack to him, he huddled under the cozy fleece blanket and white socks donned his feet.

The next day it began to drizzle as I was walking the street in midtown Atlanta. I saw, ahead of me, another homeless man on a bench, wet materials covering his head. I noticed how people passed him without even a glance. As I approached, he looked up at me and called me over to ask me if I could please bring him something to drink and a dry covering for his body. I replied that I was willing. I headed back home to my apartment and made him a sandwich, put in a new pair of socks from the package I had given Melvin earlier (contributed by Floyd, my husband). This was becoming a family "*to do.*" I had planned on keeping a pair out for myself to walk around the apartment, but they were not meant for me. Something so insignificant in value can be very rewarding to those in need.

I grabbed a bottle of water from the fridge and included the other matching blanket that I pulled out to give him as a covering. I believe that these blankets were in reserve for these two gentlemen. These items were taken to Tim, and he was happy to remove the wet covering and cover himself with a dry cuddly blanket. He immediately removed his shoes and put on dry socks.

God wants us to be attentive regarding our humility and compassion for His people in whatever state they are in. We need to learn to love the unlovable, as well as the loveable. We cannot afford to pick and choose. I found my reading pathway in Matthew 25:

> For I was hungry and you gave me something to eat, I was thirsty and you gave me something to drink, I was a stranger and you invited me in, I needed clothes and you clothed me, I was sick and you looked after me, I was in prison and you came to visit me. Then the righteous will answer him, "Lord, when did we see you hungry and feed you, or thirsty and gave you something to drink? When did we see you as a stranger and invited you in, or needing clothes did clothe you? When did we see you sick or in prison and go to visit you?" The King will reply, "Truly I tell you, whatever you did for one of the least of these brothers and sisters of mine, you did for me." (Matthew 25:35–40 NIV)

Tears of joy flood me!

I include the homeless in my prayers with a specific focus and need. I noticed that Tim would make a point to watch for me and call me over for conversation when I took a walk around the block. He asked me to pray for him. I told him I was already doing that.

One day, I thought, "Why not allow them to choose the meal they wanted to eat and not take something of my choice? I decided to give him cash. I saw his look of disbelief and his inability in knowing how to receive this kind of gift. He thanked me. I strive to treat people well as instructed in Proverbs 14: "Those who oppress the poor insult their Maker, but helping the poor honors Him" (Prov. 14:31 NLT).

My granddaughter, Makayla, observed carefully and seemed to be touched at the thought of what I was sharing with her concerning helping those who are in need of our help. She asked if she could have something to take to them also. It was good to see her compassion for others. Hopefully a seed was planted for lifelong attention to giving out of an abundant heart.

One evening I decided to order out and when my delivery came to my door it was one of the homeless men I had been praying for. He did a double take when he recognized me at about the same time.

I asked clumsily, "Aren't you the young man from across the street?"

He replied, "Yes, this is what I'm doing."

I sighed to myself, "Thank you, Jesus."

Never count God out of your equation because his numbers will never add, multiply, subtract, or divide as yours! When you trust and learn to lean on Him, you'll begin to see that the sum is far greater than its parts. In a synergistic way!

His calling me away from my home was what I thought was my desire . . . but it was He who gave me the desire of my heart to come and live in the city. The Spirit of the Lord is in your system. One day, after my settling in phase, one of the apartment managers called me to ask if she could come up because she had something to give to me. "Sure, okay." When she arrived, she presented a gift bag with two books. She was a sign from God that affirmed I was where He wanted me to be at this time. One book was authored by Bishop T.D. Jakes. She explained that she once worked for him. The other was a book by Dr. Myles Munroe. It was a divine gift.

Her face said it all when I asked her, "How did you know?"

"I just knew."

It was touching for the reason that I always quote, "He is so mindful of us!"

I am one of about twenty-three floors of apartment dwellers in a building with an estimated total of around 800—1,000 residents. However, I became the chosen of a gift of His love. I opened the book and found a quote that affirmed what I had recently shared.

I felt a call to the freedom to do above what I always desired to do. I awakened early— before sunrise—to retreat to the balcony that I might behold the moment. It was wonderful to hear how quiet it was, to enjoy the peace as though I was the only person on the planet and just take in the awe of the city, still lit from the night. I heard from within, *"The city of lights."* Now, many would not characterize Atlanta as such. They would think of the sinful nature that seemed welcomed by the masses. But God sees through His Son, Jesus Christ. Jesus is the filter of filth and sinfulness. God does not wink at sin, He hates it. But His Son paid the price on the cross by spilling His blood and the breaking of His body that we may be made whole, delivered, and set free from *"every sin that beset us"* (Heb. 12:1 KJV). It was at Calvary that He declared, "It is Finished" (John 19:30 KJV). His grace is not a permission to sin, but grace, according to Titus 2: "For the Grace of God that bringeth salvation hath appeared to all men, teaching us to deny ungodliness and worldly lusts, we should live soberly, righteously, and godly, in this present world" (Titus 2:11–12 KJV).

God sees us as his workmanship. He "spoke" us into existence as a masterful piece of art. *Poema* is of Greek origin and means "masterpiece, poem, or work of art." We matter! We are radiated as the glory of His work. That's how I felt, as I sat there speaking to Him, declaring and decreeing His Word, establishing it by faith into the earth and namely this city! He called it a city of light. That's how I will perceive it. *Atlanta Matters!* "Arise, shine, for thy light is come and the Glory of the Lord is upon us" (Isa. 60:1 KJV "Who has called us out of darkness into His marvelous Light "(1 Peter 2:9 KJV). "Let your light shine so that men may see your good works and Glorify God in Heaven" (Matt. 5:16 KJV). The people of Atlanta, this nation, and the entire universe are all in the Word concerning His glory.

As I looked to the north, south, east, and west of my building this is my description. Tall high-rises that surrounded 77 on every side. I am in the process of learning to memorize Psalm 91, which is known as the Psalm of Protection. I see the symbolism of these buildings as "a fortress, high towers" included in the Scripture from Psalm 91. My Building 77 is in the middle, so the Word comes to me saying, "He that dwelleth in the secret of the Most High, shall abide in the shadow of the Almighty." And "I will say of the Lord, He is my refuge and my fortress, in Him will I trust" (Psalm 91:1, 2 KJV). The Word in me works for me. It is personal to where we are in the Now and in the Pandemic. God is at work even now! He is Lord. He is in the midst of these high-rises. I feel His protection in this fortress, in Him will I trust!

The most opportunistic sum of these offerings is that I am having the time of my life writing, rehearsing, studying, praying, and being taught with the thought of being in His secret place.

Father, open our spiritual eyes that we may behold your presence. Sanctify our ears that we may hear the voice of You, as our Shepherd. Guard our tongue so that we may be quicker to hear and slower to speak. Block out the negative thoughts of our minds and create in us a clean heart and renew a right spirit in us. We thank You for Your angels on assignment to protect and for Your Holy Spirit to lead and guide us through all paths. "To the only

Wise God our Savior, be glory, and majesty, dominion and power forever and ever" (Jude 1:25 KJV). Amen.

God's Homework: Now is a good time to step out in faith! Purchase a small journal and write out the vision. Put your plans on paper!

58

It Works for Me

❧

ERNESTINE MEADOWS MAY

*He was mindful of us in our low estate: for His
mercy endureth forever.* (Psalm 136:23 KJV)

I believe that God has ordained men on the earth to be our protector and covering because of their physical prowess and strength. By his spiritual command, God's directive is that man loves his wife as Christ loves the church. Consider that love! A father or husband who approaches the throne of God on the behalf of his wife and family has the favor of God upon him.

Some years ago, I was feeling a strong, sharp pain in the left side of my chest that was as excruciating as a flash of lightning piercing the soft tissue in that area. Even in the shower, as the streams of water pelted against my body, it was almost unbearable to the point of screaming. *Where was this coming from? Did I have cancer? Was I going to die a slow death from it?* Fear came in many questions! Why do we always think the worse in these situations? This is the way Satan wants us to think and believe. I tried to be brave and endure the pain until such time as it would leave on its own, but it didn't. After about a week of keeping silent, I finally revealed it to my husband.

The next morning, I was released from the fear and the attachment of pain that I had been experiencing for days. I examined my body to be sure that the pain was no longer there. I let my husband know that it had gone.

He responded, so matter-of-factly, that he had prayed for me last night. "Oh! What needless pain we bear . . . all because we do not carry everything to God in prayer." The songwriter must have had a similar experience. We have no need to suffer pain, sickness, or the ravages of diseases in our body because Jesus has finished a work at the cross that promises, as written in Isaiah 53: "Surely he hath borne our griefs, and carried our sorrows: yet we did esteem him stricken, smitten of God, and afflicted. But He was wounded for our transgressions, He was bruised for our iniquities: the chastisement of our peace was upon him; and with his stripes we are healed" (Isa. 53:5 KJV).

False evidence is always from the accuser of the brethren, but I pray that your faith will hold and that you will be set free by the precious crimson blood of Jesus Christ, our Lord. Have faith in God. Because of the love of God, I can't pray enough. I can't thank Him enough. I can't speak of His goodness, mercy, and grace enough.

God's Homework: Create a prayer journal. Pray for others. When you hear of someone who has a need, record it, be sure to include the specifics and the date. God is watching and He is the rewarder of those who diligently seek Him.

59

The Visit—On Assignment

༒

SHELLEY M. FISHER, PH.D.

That at the name of Jesus every knee should bow, of those in heaven, and of those on earth, and of those under the earth and that every tongue should confess that Jesus Christ is Lord, to the glory of God the Father. (Phil. 2:10–11 KJV)

I read about a pastor/prophet who had been bedridden for almost a year. Then, he received a revelation of God's Word and began to speak healing Scriptures, aloud, over his situation. Kenneth Hagin's writings intrigued me. In his book, *The Authority of the Name of Jesus*, he tells of his illness and how he grabbed hold of God's Word and was healed. I read things in his books that I had never heard of, and I had been in the church all my life. His writings were revelatory to me. I thought about what it would be like to meet this man. I decided I would love to attend one of his meetings. Besides, my brother lived in the same area. I could visit with him.

My husband agreed to my going and my brother seemed excited to have me visit. I set my travel plans in motion—plane ticket, rental car, etc. The Kenneth Hagin Ministry was located in Broken Arrow, Oklahoma, near Tulsa. I usually try to recruit friends to travel with me, but on this occasion, I did not make any attempt to do that. I had decided to go solo and was very comfortable doing so.

My brother was glad to see me but was not interested in attending all of the meetings with me. He worked during the day and said he would plan to attend one in the evening. Each meeting was exciting, with the spiritual gifts in operation. I met people from all over the country. Kenneth Hagin displayed such humility and wisdom. Many people were healed, and many answered the call for salvation. It was as though the Bible had come alive.

I attended the meetings during the day and returned again in the evening. My brother and I were passing each other. When I awakened, he was gone to work. When I returned from the daily meetings, he would arrive home shortly afterward; then I would go out to the evening meetings again.

On my second morning in Tulsa, before leaving for the meeting, a spirit of travail came over me. My usual prayer mode is to walk and pray. This particular morning, there was also an intensity to cry and moan. I grabbed the mantle of the fireplace and prayed in the spirit as if my life depended on it. The Lord did not reveal to me the person or situation for which I was praying. This continued throughout the duration of my visit.

When I returned from the meetings at night, my brother and several friends would be in the kitchen area playing cards. They always invited me to play, but they had just the right number and I was not interested. My room was on the other side of the house. I was usually ready to go to bed to prepare for the next day. Their socializing and playing cards did not disturb me.

In the mornings, I would walk through the house praying, sensing now that this was what I was to do. Always in the living room, near that fireplace, I would become immobilized, grab hold of the mantle and cry out to God in my prayer language, praying in tongues.

My brother accompanied me to one of the evening meetings. He was being polite, but I could tell he was not really interested. I was still grateful to have his company. Meetings, returning home to card players, going to bed, and waking to pray before attending the morning meeting filled out my routine.

The week seemed to pass so quickly, as often happens when you are enjoying yourself. My brother and I found the space to have dinner one evening before my departure. He and his friends bid me farewell and safe travels.

About a month later, I received a call from his friend, Darryl. I detected something grave in his tone as he greeted me.

"I have bad news. I did not want to call your parents. Your brother has been beaten up by drug dealers, pretty badly. Your family needs to come."

When I hung up the phone, I sensed the Holy Spirit telling me that my intercessory prayer, while at my brother's home, was for his life, that he would not die. I drove to my parents' home and broke the news to them. They begin to prepare right away to make the trip to Tulsa.

I thought I was going to enjoy Kenneth Hagin, but I was on assignment. I did not see any signs of drugs in my brother's home or among his friend as they'd played cards. I believe the intercessory prayer saved his life. The Word in Job says, "He will deliver even one who is not innocent through the cleanness of your hands" (Job 22:30 NKJV).

God's Homework: God may give you an unusual assignment which you may not understand until days later. You may think you are focusing on one thing, but God is putting His plan in motion through you. Listen to His voice and obey Him. He just needs you to be a willing vessel.

60

Pray for the Men

SHELLEY M. FISHER, PH.D.

He will even deliver the one [for whom you intercede]
who is not innocent; yes, he will be delivered through
the cleanness of your hands. (Job 22:30 AMP)

During times of intercession, I have received instructions from the Lord. During this instance, I was told to "pray for the men." I thought this was an interesting directive. Quite frankly, I wanted to make sure I was hearing from God and that these were not my thoughts. It was not long before I received a confirmation.

I attended a prayer breakfast in my community and the guest preachers were men from a nearby major city. There were about three hundred people in attendance. The praise and worship were refreshing. One of the prophets began to prophesy. The other prophet began to walk out in the audience.

When he came to my table, he pointed at me and said, "You, you will pray for the men when no one else will."

That was confirmation number one.

Some friends and I used to go to a Wednesday service in a nearby community. The majority ministry gifts were prophets and would engage in presbytery, speaking edifying words to the congregants. My friends stopped attending, but I continued and felt that God was calling me to this fellowship. I felt drawn to this church, but a part of me wondered why. The pastor was Italian.

I know "God is no respecter of persons" (Acts 10:34 NKJV). I wanted to know what God was doing.

One evening the pastor announced he had a ministry specific to the black male; this was an assignment the Lord had given him. This was my second confirmation. The Lord put me with a pastor who had an identical assignment. For years, praying for men was a major focus of my intercession. While at this church, I was mentored in my prophetic gift. God has a way of getting us to where He wants us. Place and race are not God's requisites.

Jeremiah 29 "For I know the plans I have for you," declares the Lord, plans to prosper you and not to harm you, plans to give you hope and a future" (Jer. 29:11 NKJV).

God's Homework: God makes divine connections bringing re-enforcement to you. He wants you to be willing and obedient; then He will do the rest. Are you open to different cultures where God may assign you? How will you respond when the assignment is not likely something you are interested in, nor the culture for which you are accustomed? God has a plan and assignment for you. Position yourself to receive and move forward.

61

Let There Be Light

GLORIA SHARPE SMITH

Therefore I tell you, whatever you ask for in prayer, believe that you have received it, and it will be yours. (Mark 11:24 NIV)

Have you ever uttered to yourself or others, "Well, all I can do is pray?"

I'm sure, just like me, you probably have. Before I had genuine experiences with answered prayers, I said it rather often. As my prayer life matured over the years, I learned that, while prayer is a powerful weapon against adversity, it is comforting as well. For me, it's a simple act of communicating with God. It has become my first line of action in every situation.

It was on a Wednesday night, after Bible study, that my faith and the power of prayer were tested. The Bible lesson we studied was not the event that caused me to call on God and pray earnestly for our safety, using a faith that was intentional, bold, and extremely sincere. It was an evening neither I, nor my then-ten-year-old granddaughter, Lexxus, has ever forgotten.

It was very common for my husband and me to attend Wednesday night Bible study at our church in Gary, Indiana. On this particular summer night, our granddaughter was with us. She frequently spent time during the summer with us and we enjoyed every minute of our time together.

We headed to the car for the ride home. My husband was driving. I was sitting in the front, next to him, and Lexxus was safely buckled in the back. The location of the church was in close proximity to a heavily traveled highway. Out of nowhere, large drops of rain began to hit the windshield, producing a sound that was loud and rhythmic. We could also hear the howling of the wind and felt its power. The car seemed to be swishing about from right to left, with no regard for anyone or anything. Objects were flying across our path. *Where did this monster come from? Why didn't either of us know it was in the area?* There was no warning. We were in a bad downpour. Thunder and lightning were on the scene. Visibility was almost gone. We couldn't see anything outside of the windows, except for a few cars that had pulled over and the faint headlights from cars on the other side of the freeway. I asked my husband to pull over. He promptly admitted that it wasn't safe to do so because he couldn't see the embankment. I understood. It was obvious that something scary and very intense was going on.

Lexxus, who had been sitting quietly in the back, began to whimper out of fear. I told her that we were going to be just fine. I further added that God would keep us safe. I could tell my statement of faith wasn't very comforting to her. *What else should I do?* As my husband continued to concentrate on driving, I unbuckled my seatbelt and maneuvered my way onto the backseat. It was an awkward struggle but well worth it. I could tell she wanted me beside her. While holding her close, I began to pray, purposefully out loud, for our safety. We were all terrified and had never been in a storm of this magnitude.

I had no doubt that God was hearing my prayers, however, I desperately wanted my sweet Lexxus to witness how He always hears and answers. I prayed all the way home. Our route took us by a popular, and usually well-lit, truck stop. But, on this particular night, all was pitch black and scary. Even the streetlights were out.

I continued my prayer out loud so that Lexxus could hear me.

"Lord, please show Lexxus that You are real and that You love her and want to keep us safe. When we get home, please let our lights be on, so that we can see. I ask this in Jesus' Name. Amen!"

I kept assuring her that everything was going to be just fine.

"I hope so," she said, "I'm scared."

After that, she began to quiet down, but I must confess that I didn't quite have "perfect peace" either. In all, we'd traveled about an hour. We noticed that the houses on our route were also without light. *What was the condition of our lights?* I believed they were one hundred percent functional. My faith was being tested and I knew it. I wanted to pass the test. I also believed God wanted Lexxus to get to know Him and experience the knowledge of the power of prayer. I realized only now that I was attempting to fulfill Scripture. "Train up a child in the way he should go: and when he is old, he will not depart from it" (Prov. 22:6 KJV). We were in a situation that I called, "A teachable moment."

Our fear, in the midst of this storm, called for action. My husband's driving skills were remarkable that night. It was such a sweet relief to move out of the storm and get even closer to home. As we approached our street, my heart was racing. The lights in our home were set on timers that, pretty much, always worked perfectly. On this night, nothing had changed. As we turned the corner, there were lights glowing through the windows of our house! It was radiant and a welcome sight. Amazingly, ours was the *only* home on the street that had light.

We were home, safe, and thankful; just in time to catch the local news and hear the evening weather report. It was then that we learned that the storm was actually a tornado that had touched down in the area. We were kept safe that Wednesday night, but just as important, our light gave witness to the mind of a sweet young girl who would grow up knowing that God answers prayer!

God's Homework: Hug someone and whisper a prayer in his/her ear! Also, let a child hear you pray.

62

The Simplicity of Believing in Prayer

∽✦∽

AS TOLD TO ERNESTINE MEADOWS MAY
BY HER HUSBAND, FLOYD MAY

Cast all your anxiety on Him because He cares...
(1 Peter 5:7 NIV)

I want to tell you about how God wants to be a part of our everyday living. He's not just there for the big requests and needs, but He cares about the small, mindful things. I have loved and participated in bowling for over fifty years. In one particular instance, I was having a bad dayS at it. To be honest, my whole season had been off. As you might know, there are many variables in the game. Experience has taught me that my timing was not what it should have been. I considered timing to be a major factor in having a successful bowling game. I couldn't figure out how to get my game in sync. Everything I adjusted and practiced was not yielding the score I wanted. I had always been proud of the fact that my timing was usually good.

I went through an entire season in this condition. I was bowling in three different leagues and practicing a lot on the side, but I never regained my timing that year. I never thought to ask God to help me with my problem. After all, He had greater requests to answer. So, I continued to try to fix it on my own.

After the winter season ended, two of my friends and I decided to travel to Cincinnati, Ohio, to bowl in a tournament. My friends were doubles partners for the tournament. I had no partner but was paired with another gentleman who needed a partner also. My bowling was bad. My high game was only 172, when my average had been 206. You can imagine how badly I felt. Added to this disappointment was an issue with my wrist, which was hurting badly. It got to the point where I couldn't see how I would be able to bowl in the next event, which was now only two hours away. My two friends decided to bowl another set of doubles. While they were bowling, I went and sat in the lounge, still trying to figure out why my bowling game was so bad. As I was sitting there, God spoke to me inwardly to say, *"You are presenting your ball too low."* Never would I have thought God would help me with my bowling game. When He spoke, I jumped up off of the stool where I was sitting and went out on the faraway alley to go through a dry run of my bowling approach. I had to test this out!

For the first time all that season I realized how I had let my ball fall lower on my approach. In doing this, I had to raise my ball to the level of the swing position and that is what had thrown off my timing. I had to compensate for the push away to go into my back-swing and balance that momentum. This had been my problem and had not been a part of my normal routine, so adding this element of the process caused my timing to be off. Good bowlers know that, sometimes, when you're trying to correct yourself, you really haven't paid attention to that one thing that has thrown you off unless someone makes you aware of it. Now, after the Lord made me aware of what I was doing wrong, I took to the lanes with excitement. My first game in the next event concluded with a score of 272! I was taught a two-fold lesson that day. He wanted to be a part of everything I did, and I learned that I should not lean on my own understanding. Lesson well taken!

Father, I thank You for being so very mindful of everything that concerns us. I thank you that you said in your word, "Before they call, I will answer; while they are still speaking, I will hear" (Isa. 65:24 KJV). Father, You are awesome in all Your ways. May we all know the love and care You have for those who are called by Your Name! Amen.

God's Homework: Is there someone you can join with to agree as one in prayer? God promises to be in the midst of two or three who pray in agreement. Choose a time when each of you can stop daily activities and pray for a moment as a team.

63

Prayer Is Essential

༺✦༻

AS TOLD TO ERNESTINE MEADOWS MAY
BY HER COUSIN, LOLA SAXTON WAINWRIGHT

*Now faith is the substance of things hoped for in the
evidence of things not seen.* (Hebrew 11:1 KJV)

In the early 1980's, my husband suddenly passed. Needless to say,
we were all very devastated. My eighteen-year-old son was soon
to be graduating from high school. He had recently informed me
that his girlfriend was pregnant and that he was the father of the
child. I was heartbroken. He also let me know that there would
be major changes to his plans after high school. He would not be
going to college but would, instead, enlist in the U.S. Air Force.
He planned to marry his girlfriend. They would move away. We
had many long talks, as we processed all of his options, but in the
end his mind was made up.

I cried and prayed a lot. I was grieving the loss of my husband,
compounded with the news that my son was bringing to me now. I
wished that my husband could be with me to help us through this.

I had not been strong in my faith, but in recent years, I had
strayed away from the church and did not attend regularly. My
best friend, Von, invited me to her church. I started attending
there. She told me to put all my troubles in God's hands. Although
things were not perfect, I started to feel better about my situation. My son and his fiancé were married. They moved to Arizona,

where he was stationed in the Air Force. Six months later I had a healthy grandson. Sadly, their marriage did not survive. My son remained in the Air Force for a few years longer and received his college degree. I am so grateful for Von inviting me back to church. My son has remarried. I now enjoy four beautiful grandchildren.

My advice for anyone going through a crisis in life is simple. When it seems as though you cannot see a way out of the situation, trust and believe in God. He will surely answer your prayer if you believe. I now know more than ever concerning the power of prayer by faith. God will bring me through anything that comes my way. He has shown me how my faith increases as I believe.

God's Homework: Call your cousin, your best friend, or your sister/brother and talk with them about something very positive that has happened in your life.

64

Tommy Tom

SHELLEY M. FISHER, PH.D.

Train up a child in the way he should go, and when he
is old, he will not depart from it. (Prov. 22:6 KJV)

I do not think teachers realize the impressions they make upon their students. I continue to learn how I have impacted students. I can remember being at an event at my church when a young lady came to me, introducing herself, saying I was her instructor in the fifth grade. She also said, as a child, she always wanted to be just like me.

She continued, "I liked the way you dressed, especially those slingback heels."

I thought to myself, "*If you only knew . . . my heels are so narrow that those were the only shoes I could keep on my feet.*"

Students compartmentalize what they like about you.

Another student told me about the favorite things he remembered that we did in class. His best were to make candles and fudge while studying solids, liquids, and gasses. My most outstanding memory surrounds a student who is now a school principal. I will call him Tommy Tom. He and I had reconnected on Facebook. He told me he sat near my desk and I allowed him to stay after class to clean the chalkboard. He said he thought he was my favorite, until later on, he realized that I had treated all of my students the same.

Tommy Tom shared that his mother was bipolar, and he went through a lot at home. But when he came to school, I made him feel important. His parents laid a strong spiritual foundation in him. He has had many challenges and overcome them all. God brought him through many adverse situations. He now helps others. I went to hear him do a presentation to a youth group at a local church. He has a gift for dealing with disillusioned and disenfranchised youth.

I invited him to address a graduating class. Before I arrived to meet him, he entertained the staff with a story I had heard from him recently. It seems I invited him to my church. My husband and I were renewing our vows. He did not realize I had a husband. He said he was crushed because he wanted to marry me. We still laugh about this today.

As leaders executing everyday tasks, the way we treat people is important because we are making lasting impressions. As we interact with people, we are making deposits in their lives. We want to impart positivity to help people reach their destiny.

Young minds are impressionable. I thank God for allowing me to touch the lives of so many of our children. He has always been with me. Back then, I did not have the wisdom that I have today, however, I believe teaching and administration were ordained for me even before I realized it. God walked me through the classroom of life. To God be the glory for the things He has done.

God's Homework: You do not know what impression you are making on people. It behooves you to be kind and nurturing, for you could be entertaining angels unawares. Allow God to deposit Himself in you so that you can deposit into his people.

65

Stop the Crime

SHELLEY M. FISHER, PH.D.

By the blessings of the upright, the city is exalted.
(Prov. 11:11 KJV)

Our city was riddled with crime. We were in the headlines across the country: Gary, Indiana, "Murder Capital of the United States." Newscasters allowed the words to roll off their lips as though it were the city's official name.

Those of us who believe in the power of God were provoked to do something about this. After all, the Word says to "speak to the mountain and it shall be removed" (Mark 11:23 author's paraphrase). A member of Gary Educators for Christ, Rita Byron, suggested that we begin to pray to remove the title that had been ascribed to our city. I do not recall the details in the planning, but our group prayed on Saturday mornings for one year with consistency and persistence. We prayed like clockwork, not missing a beat, remaining faithful to our assignment to decrease crime and murder. It did not matter whether it was rain, snow, or sleet, we were at the educator's building, praying every Saturday morning, expecting to receive results.

I can remember one Saturday where the Lord encouraged us with these words: "*While you are doing My work, praying for My people, I will take care of your business and bless you; and as you pray for all children, I will take care of yours.*"

As these words flowed from my lips, it was as if the Lord was saying, *"Do not worry about the time spent thinking you could be doing other things, for I will redeem your time by attending to your business and those things that concern you."*

I had forgotten about this prophecy until in recent years my co-author, Ernestine, reminded me of it. She relates how her children have always been blessed when others may have not gotten a position or acquired something. Her children have always been blessed in various circumstances, and even today, God continues to promote them to the highest levels of position in their employment. The central theme throughout all of our experiences has been to trust God!

I, too, can attest to this for my children as well. Whether their concern is a job, a position, or healing from an illness, they've continued to be blessed. Those Saturday morning prayer sessions for our city were like putting spiritual money in the bank of God. He has given us withdrawals that have persisted well into the future. When we take care of God's business, He will take care of our business.

We came together from different backgrounds and religious teachings, but we meshed into the mind of God to get His will done on the earth. The headlines one year later were different. They read that the crime rate had decreased in Gary, Indiana, citing statistics. We were overjoyed to see actual proof of an answer to our prayer for our city.

Even as we committed to pray for our nation, families, schools, churches, marriages, and those in authority, we were also amazed to see results of our school district's test scores, which were considerably higher as well.

We prayed, believing that God would do what He said He would do and give us the desires of our heart, which was to have a safe city with diminishing crime. We could have stayed inside of our various homes, lamenting about how terrible the crime was or blasting city officials, but we were moved to action. The Word says: "By the blessings of the upright the city is exalted" (Prov. 11:11 NKJ). We blessed our city, declaring it to be a beacon of light on a hill, drawing men, women, boys, and girls to Jesus. We were faithful in pursuit of God's blessings over our city, and He was faithful to honor our desire to reduce crime.

He is still faithful to us today. I believe those prayers were a sweet savor in God's nostrils, and He is still blessing me and others in the group who do His work. Each of the participants in that Saturday prayer group would probably have a testimony to attest to God's continuing to bless us. His Word declares, "I watch over my word to perform it, and none of my words return void, but accomplish that which I please and prospers in the thing whereto I sent it" (Isa. 55:11 NKJ).

God made us to serve both Him and others. He tells us to go into the world and preach the gospel to every creature (Matt.28:16–20 KJV). We are to be disciples and spread the Word. That, of course, is witnessing for Jesus, praying, and performing acts that will lead people to salvation. Our small group changed the direction of our city.

We gave no place to the enemy. The Word says that one will put a 1000 to flight and two will put 10,000 to flight (Deut. 32:30 author's paraphrase). If men could come together in one accord, what power would be exhibited to change circumstances in our communities, businesses, and racial equality? I believe that with behavioral changes within the body of Christ there would be character changes that would make us enablers to do the work of the ministry.

God is a "rewarder of those who diligently seek Him" (Heb. 11:6 NLT). He tells us to: "Seek Him with all our heart" (Jer. 29:13 NLT). While we are seeking, He changes us to look more like Him. While our Saturday group was praying for the city, we prayed God's Word. He was faithful to answer according to Isaiah 54:11 (NKJV). Seek God so you can move in the spirit and not in self. The Word will stretch and enlarge you so that you will be receptive and not stuck in your thoughts. God changed us as we prayed for the city and taught us this valuable lesson— that as we take care of His business, He will take care of our business. Trust God!

God's Homework: "God is a Spirit and those who worship Him must worship Him in spirit and in truth" (John 4:24 KJV); praying is worshiping God in spirit and in truth. The Lord wants us to intercede so that He can get His will done on the earth. Ezekiel 22 says, " And I sought for a man among them, that should make up the hedge, and stand in the gap before me for the land, that I should not destroy it: but I found none" (Ezek.22:30 KJV). Make yourself available to answer the call to prayer and be that change to get God's will done on the earth.

66

School Business

∾⚬∾

ERNESTINE MEADOWS MAY

And we know that for those who love God all things
work together for good, for those who are called
according to his purpose. (Rom. 8:28 ESV)

An evaluation of a cadre of teachers in the Montessori Methods at our Pre-School was about to happen. The school's director and her appointed staff would visit us after attending classes for over 3,000 required hours at a location in Illinois. Our practicum would prove whether or not we would receive certification after this evaluative process.

It was a time to be nervous and anxious. We would be performing on stage with our students before an audience who would decide our prowess in the philosophy of educating primary students. My classroom aide had been well trained by me. Her skills in observation were very keen indeed. She loved this method of training children in self-discipline and independent learning as much as I did. I had prayed that the children would be focused and would be at peace as they selected their work and embraced it until completion. I also prayed that order was followed, as they had been instructed as a daily part of their daily experience.

On the day of the visit, the director of Meca-Seton Training Center and her staff came to our classroom. I welcomed them to our world. They wanted to be left to the task of observation. I retired to a position on the floor out of everyone's distractive eyes. I immediately began to see a sight unfold that I had never seen before. The children, a mixed population of ages ranging from three to five, were moving about quietly, selecting their work and making decisions as to their level of interest. They were then sitting at their choice of tables, carrying mats to the floor to work, selecting sensorial materials, cultural learning activities, and practical life tasks in language, science, or math. They were focused and immersed in individual and shared learning styles. The children made very selective choices for their age-appropriate levels.

I was watching everything with my natural eyes, but also there was a spiritual visitation that I could not dismiss. I was seeing the children in a room touched by a mist. It hovered and lingered until the end of the observation period and then it lifted. God was letting me know that my prayer had been answered.

The Meca-Seton staff walked around the room in strict observation, as the director of Meca-Seton remained at the door to scan the environment and see everyone and everything in its rightful place, as it had been demonstrated.

- Order (check)
- Independence (check)
- Motivation (check)
- Responsibility (check)
- Self-care (check)
- Coordination (check)
- Focused (check)

One of the students came over to where I was sitting to read the story of *The Three Bears*. The action did not go unnoticed! Bianca was at the easel painting. The staff member watched her from a distance, noticing each step of the process: clipping a sheet of art paper to the board at the easel, securing the colors of paint she wanted to use, getting a cup of water to clean the brush and a sponge to dab the brush dry after washing it. These were the steps that had been taught to her. When she completed her work, she moved it to the drying area and cleaned up for the next person to use the area. Those are the signs of Montessori training methods. It is the picture the Meca-Seton staff were looking for—a well provided selection of materials and proper training for the success of children.

All of the characteristics of a Montessori environment were being displayed and unfolded during the entire morning visit. I sat there, almost in disbelief, as every one of the children performed what had been taught in a self-guided community. They went about making their teacher and classroom aide proud of the seamless, easy flowing and peaceful co-existence of little people.

At the end of the day, and after all Montessori teachers had been observed and evaluated, the institute's director returned to my classroom with a good report. She stated that what she was about to do did not usually happen. I had passed with flying colors to the point of her presenting me with a certificate on the spot. I knew that the children, under the unction of the Holy Spirit, had enabled me to receive it. I passed! She also stated that the children seemed to really enjoy their work. She even noticed that the children had not once asked about going outside for play.

I would normally have an end-of-day chat with my wonderful classroom aide concerning planning and management. On this day we talked about how the children worked to a level and degree we had not even once experienced.

She surprisingly said, "I prayed for them."

How could God not honor us? We had both prayed for the same things. It is a promise from God, found in Matthew 18: "Again, I say unto you, that if two of you shall agree on earth as touching anything that they shall ask, it shall be done for them of my Father which is in heaven" (Matt. 18:19 KJV). And there it is! Choose a like-minded believer to agree with you in prayer that your Father in heaven may honor you with answered prayer. Prayer works!

God's Homework: Prayer is a huge part of on-the-job training. Do not cease to pray for your workplace. Make it a habit to pray for the business and your coworkers daily.

67

Your Tie Tack Is Missing

GLORIA SHARPE SMITH

*Bring ye all the tithes into the storehouse, that there may be meat
in mine house, and prove me now herewith, says the Lord of hosts,
if I will not open you the windows of heaven, and pour you out a
blessing, that there shall not be room enough to receive it. And I
will rebuke the devourer for your sakes . . .* (Mal. 3:10–11a KJV)

Sundays were always a special time for my husband Ernest and
me. This particular Sunday was no different. We had attended
our regular morning worship service and our spiritual needs had
been met. Afterwards, it was customary for us to go to one of our
favorite, local restaurants for brunch. I enjoyed having a delicious
meal that I didn't have to prepare. This life-pause also afforded us
the opportunity to have quality time and catch up on what had
taken place during the week that was behind us.

While enjoying our meal, I noticed his necktie. There was
absolutely nothing in the exact spot where an 18-karat gold tie
tack had been when we had left home. I had purchased the tie
tack for him while on one of my trips to Egypt. I'd spent countless hours in various specialty shops seeking the perfect souvenir
for him. The shopping ended when I settled on a tie tack crafted
with precision, custom-made and bearing his initials in Egyptian
hieroglyphics. The designer was elated that I had chosen him to

create this fine piece of jewelry and that it would be worn by an American.

In turn, my husband was very appreciative and delighted that I had chosen such a thoughtful and practical gift. He wore a tie to work daily. Tie clips and tacks were essential accessories to compliment his wardrobe. Because this particular tie tack was special to him, he wore it most often on Sundays.

When I noticed that it was missing my heart sank.

I looked at him and said, "Your tie tack is missing!"

I can only imagine the look that he saw on my face. Immediately, I saw a mirrored and corresponding grimace on his face. The meal that we had been enjoying was over. Our disposition had changed from pleasurable contentment to sadness and disbelief.

I've always been a faithful tither. My thoughts went to that portion of Malachi 3 which says, "I will rebuke the devour for your sakes" (Mal. 3:11). I thought, *"Lord, you can't let this happen. This cannot be."* At that very moment, I felt I had to say a quick, silent prayer. I have learned that the length of a prayer does not matter to God. I simply mouthed these simple words, *"Lord, You can't let this happen. This cannot be. Please let the tie tack to be found. You know where it is. I believe Your Word and I'm acting on it."*

I suggested to my husband that we backtrack. "Let's go back to the church and see if we can get in and look for it before we go home."

My husband paid for the meal and we began our search. We started right there in our immediate area and then graduated out to the car. We were looking for a very small, but, in some ways priceless, piece of significance that was personalized just for him. Our search of the car was equally disappointing. We rode in silence to the church and in my mind, I was desperately pleading for God to prove His word. I longed for the opportunity to brag on His faithfulness, regarding His word.

Being a tither gives me the assurance that all I've been given stewardship over is covered and protected from destruction, because it essentially belongs to Him. I was waiting for God to reward both my obedience in tithing and my faith. My husband drove onto the church parking lot and pulled into the exact spot where we had previously parked. This time, however, he parked facing the opposite direction. I was hoping that the security guard would still be on duty and that he would give us access into the building. Although the tie tack was small—about the size of a dime—I wanted to believe it could be easily spotted.

We were ready to trace every step that he had taken prior to leaving the church that morning. I remember eagerly opening the car door to get out. My eyes instantly captured the image that had taken my breath away in sadness just a short while earlier. There it was. The 18-karat gold, Egyptian cartouche tie tack lay untouched and waiting for its owner.

"Ernest," I exclaimed! "Here it is! And look! It's not even damaged! Not a single car has driven over it, and no one has stepped on it. It's perfect!"

I stooped down and picked up the tie tack, all the while saying, "Thank you, Jesus!"

My husband was thrilled and grateful that I had encouraged him to go back to the church to continue the search. He thanked me for having the faith to believe and apply Scripture, proving that God honors His word and rewards our obedience and faith. Not all stories have such happy endings; however, I'm so grateful to be able to encourage, inspire, and give witness to the power of prayer, faith, obedience and, most importantly, God's faithfulness to His word.

I am reminded of another verse that we were honored to live. "Delight thyself also in the Lord; and he shall give thee the desires of thine heart" (Ps. 37:4 KJV). In other words, seek and trust the whole counsel of the Word of God. You won't be disappointed.

God's Homework: It may be difficult but take a step and trust God by committing to a regular tithing schedule.

Prayers

68

Prayer for Fathers

DORETHA STURGIS ROUSE

Father God, in the name of Jesus, we bless your name today. We thank you for fathers, putting them in place as part of the family unit. We are thankful for them watching over their children, and also lifting up all children of the world in prayer. Thank you that they give provision for their families without shrinking their duties and responsibilities in the household. Thank you, Father, for being the ultimate head of the family. Thank you for encouraging fathers to be the best that they can be for their loved ones.

We pray that earthly fathers will draw near unto their heavenly Father so that they are in relationship with you, and therefore, will model to the world those same characteristics that you possess. Father, we thank you for natural fathers who are the carriers of the seed, implanting the seed, and watching for it to grow and bring forth a good harvest.

We thank you that the natural father is the guard on the door, refusing to let ungodly things inside, but that he prays a hedge of protection for his family, keeping his family nourished and meeting their needs, both naturally and spiritually. We thank you that our fathers are providers because you give provision for us all. We revere the natural father. He is full of wisdom and might, because you are the giver of wisdom freely to those who ask of it. The natural father is a stalwart against the enemy as he studies the word that causes him to be bold and courageous. The natural father receives instruction and discipline from his heavenly Father who is always loving and caring.

Thank you, Father God, for helping the fatherless, the weak, and disenfranchised. Heavenly Father, you are the source of all life and teach natural fathers how to live in reliance upon you. In you there are many entities—love, correction, wisdom, and faith. Life begins with our relationship with you. We declare that natural fathers are to imitate your love and majesty in serving their families and mankind. Father God, we thank you for natural fathers who nurture their families and serve mankind. In the name of Jesus. Amen.

69

Friend of God Prayer

DORETHA STURGIS ROUSE

Father God, it is in the name of Jesus, Lord, we lift up your name today, we do thank you and magnify your name God for being a God who is patient and loving. God, we thank you today that you are a wonderful God. We thank you for watching over your word to perform it on our behalf. God, we thank you that you go in before us as we pray for friendships and relationships between friends, those who are bound and knitted together in you to be of help to one another. We thank you that sometimes friends disagree but always come back together and extend hands and words of courtesy. We thank you, Lord, that it is you who bind friends to make a friendship. God, we thank you for loving correction. I thank you that we are riding in the same boat because you are the captain. I thank you that no weapon formed against us shall prosper, and every lying tongue that rises up against us we as friends, shall condemn it in the name of Jesus. I thank you, Lord, that you hold us together with the glue of the Holy Ghost. I thank you as we attempt to walk together in agreement with you and know that, if we walk out of agreement with you, we thank you that we make our corrections according to you, Lord. I thank you that friends can trust you and not be without help because you said you would never leave us or forsake us. The thing that makes us friends is that we are ever connected with you in the name of Jesus.

I thank you that we can say, "I am a friend of God" that I can shout, "I AM A FRIEND OF GOD"! So Lord, we are so thankful that we are connected to you with our friends. You are the link, God. Now we give unto you friends who are reading and praying this prayer in agreement with us, that you restore friendships and bind us all together in your love. We speak truth, encouragement, and correction in love. I thank you that we copy friendship from you because you are a friend to us all. You love us with an everlasting and unconditional love. I thank you Lord that we can say, *"I am a friend of God, He is my friend,"* in Jesus' name. Amen.

70

Prayer for the Supernatural

❧

DORETHA STURGIS ROUSE

Father God, in the name of Jesus, we thank you for the supernatural and for the supernatural encounters, God, that you have allowed us to participate in. We thank you that what you allow us to do is beyond the natural—above and beyond! We pray that we have encounters with you that will puzzle the natural, and for it, Lord, I bless your name.

I thank you that encounters will come to different people, languages, races, and different cultures. Oh God, as we prepare to surrender ourselves, I thank you that the supernatural comes unexpectedly, not that we look to find it but that it shows up. That is how it is, we're not able to define it nor can we find it, but you allow us to have it, and we open up to experience it. For this, God, I thank you! We embrace the spirit to control us as we find ourselves stumbling and even fumbling to explain it, but you control it.

We cannot explain God. We cannot contain God. We can honor and worship God. He is beyond the natural mind. That is why we bless you, Lord. Thank you for the words and experience you have given your people. I thank you that it has just begun, because there is no ending to you or your super-ness. There's no ending to your ways. I thank you Lord that you have willing vessels. We ask you to come in, God, and show us what to do and how to do and recognize that the supernatural goes far beyond what science says.

Father, I pray that you visit every home, our families and those who they encounter, for they come carrying you and are being carried by you, God. I bless your name today and pray that you watch over your word to perform it. You said, "Call on me and I will answer and show you great and mighty works that you knew not." We believe great and mighty works are supernatural. Some are explainable, some we trust you to reveal to us in your moment of time. But we can surely say, as we scratch our heads, "Thank you, Jesus!"

Thank you, Lord. Thank you, Jesus. Thank you for the supernatural things that happen in our homes. Lord, you are awesome! I bless you, Lord. Even as we go into strange places, we're not expecting anything and not going in to experience the supernatural, but the *super-* shows up on the *-natural* all the time. We pray that the people will be blessed with your presence. I glorify you. I bless your name and I thank you for visitations, dreams, and visions. In your visitations, eyes will be wide open. I thank you that your super will come into our natural and take us to that place in you! Glory! Glory! Glory! In Jesus' name. Amen.

71

Prayer for Giving and Provision

～✕～

DORETHA STURGIS ROUSE

Father God, in the name of Jesus we give you glory. We praise you and we thank you. We bless your name and thank you for being the one who provides. We thank you for calling us in different languages. We can call on you in any nation and you show up and show off.

Thank you for being with children in foreign nations and with young people. God, we thank you that you put your spirit in the hearts of the ladies that you sent to Russia, and we bless your name. There are no limits to you. Thank you for using these ladies as vessels, and we thank you for their yielding. We thank you for being in Russia. Thank you for being in every language. Your Word is in your people, and it travels throughout the nations. You are the omnipresent God. You are everywhere!

Father, we thank you for the provision—for shoes. You make all things beautiful. Thank you for letting us walk in your shoes, shoes of power. Thank you for blessing the generations, and this generation. Father, thank you for a dress made in England, traveling from America to Russia. Thank you, Lord, for watching over your word to perform it. Lord, you provide. You always keep your word, your promises.

Thank you for the way you are uniting people across the world in foreign countries. I thank you that nothing or no one is foreign to you. Lord, you can be found in high mountains and deep valleys and aboard airplanes, boats, and ships as they travel the world.

Father, you live in cotton fields. You live in Russia. You match gifts and talents with your assignment. Thank you, Lord, that the Word works. Thank you for pouring your Word into those who love you. Father, we bless those who have been touched by you, and pray that they may pass the blessings on to others.

May we continue to do what you've called us to do. You are beyond our thoughts and we keep reaching higher for you. We have faith to believe that you will do what you say you will do. We thank you for your presence in every situation. Father, we thank you for watching over your word to perform it. Thank you for loving us, guiding us, and protecting us. In Jesus' name. Amen.

72

A Pandemic Prayer

❧

DORETHA STURGIS ROUSE

Father God, In the name of Jesus, we bless your name today, Lord. We are so grateful to you, God, for who you are. We are in a situation, God, that we are unfamiliar with and we don't know what to do, not knowing what's going on in this so-called pandemic world, but we thank you, God. We ask you to guide us through the dark places, in the unknown places. We thank you for being with us to help us to see the unseen and to see it through your eyes, God. Lord, we pray for strength, courage, and wisdom.

I thank you that you will use this time to minister to others and encourage others in a dark place and in an unknown place, God. We trust you to walk with us in that place of darkness and we are not so far away that we are not seeing you because we want to hold on to you. We thank you that your Word works. You have already told us to *call on you and you will answer us and show us great and mighty things that we knew not.*

We thank you for the light of your presence that shines in darkness because in you there is no darkness. God, I bless your name today! I thank you, Lord, as the world seems to be in turmoil, but we will follow your lead into a plain path, a path that you will lay out for us, God. I thank you for your words of wisdom. You encourage us at this time, and you bless our hands that we may give to others, that the fruit of your Word will feed others at this time.

I thank you that this is not a surprise to you, for you know what is going on when we don't know the end from the beginning. We trust you, God!

I pray for those who are discouraged and feel lost. I pray that you would lead us to someone who we can lift us up and encourage us with the promises of your Word. You said in your Word that "lo, I am with you always, even to the end of the world" (Matt. 28:20). We thank you, Lord, how you are using us, even in these dark times you are showing yourself bright and strong. I thank you that these words that are written show your presence. You're moving in place, for in you all darkness is dispelled. We pray for those who are stressed, worrying, and not finding their need on their own . . . but, God, you are our source, our help in our time of need.

We thank you, God, that you have us on an assignment to be the light during this time. We thank you that we let our light shine so that men may see our good works and glorify you in heaven. We thank you that we are searching for someone to bless, someone whose hand we can hold, and words we can use to edify.

We thank you that even through these times you are showing us yourself in a marvelous way. We may be in a pandemic not knowing which way is up or which way is down, but we do know who controls it and we trust you as we hear your voice, obey your voice, and move when you say move, God. I thank you that you send us into new places to do exceedingly with new people to do new things that we have not done before, because you have ordered them.

Lord, we thank you for the people who are being saved during this pandemic while praying that the souls of those lost are being found. We are here to share you as we have never shared you before. We reach out to old and young, rich and poor, people on the street, in high places and those down below during this time of distress, anger, and bitterness, we release your Word of hope, faith, and overcoming as we are your representatives.

I pray for your anointing on these writers. I thank you that you will visit them in dreams, visions, and will have encounters with them and that you will be with them to cast out all fear, doubt, and unbelief, in the name of Jesus.

During this pandemic we are not going to have pandemonium for we are rooted, grounded, and anchored in you. We shall not be moved by what we see, feel, or hear for we shall believe the report of the Lord. We believe your Word as you've said in the verses of Exodus, "I *am your Lord,* I am the Lord that heals thee, I send my word to you to bless you and to fulfill my will in the earth."

I thank you for their writings that words will come more abundantly as though a fire is set on the inside, burning with expectancy to write as never before the things you have set forth for them. Finding a need to write about a good God during a bad time. Touch their hands as they write, place clarity in their minds, give them strength, put love in their hearts, run in their feet, and everyone that they touch will be the touch of your hand. I thank you for encouraging them, giving them the *pen of the ready writer,* lifting them up, and putting a smile on their faces wherever they may go.

Lord, I thank you that you were not caught not knowing what is going on today. You are our omnipotent, all-knowing God! I speak to the north, south, east and west parts of the earth, we don't speak their language, but you do. *I am your God. Call on me.*

We pray for the president of these United States that he may be a leader full of wisdom, and divine purpose for the good of our country. Thank you for our health workers who are obedient to the call of the front line in helping others and for all who are in authority. Bless them we pray, as we give you thanks. In Jesus' name. Amen.

73

Prayer for Fathers

❧

SHELLEY M FISHER, PH.D.

Father, we thank you for being Lord of all. Thank you for ordaining Abraham to be the Father of Nations. We are grateful to be of the seed of Abraham.

Father, we believe the spirit of Elijah is in the earth turning the hearts of the fathers to the children and the hearts of the children to their fathers (Mal. 4:4–6). We pray that the voice of the prophets will cause the prodigals to return to their fathers. Father, we ask you to raise the compassion level of the fathers. Give them the grace to love and care for their children.

Lord Jesus, touch the hearts of fathers so they will not provoke or discourage their children (Col. 3:21). We ask that you give fathers the wisdom they need to raise, support, and correct their children. Manifest yourself as master teacher to fathers so they will emulate you in their dealings with their children. Cause fathers to seek your guidance for raising their children.

We pray that children will understand that rebukes, chastisement, and corrections are done in love (Prov. 3:12). We thank you for giving family members endurance and this endurance will bring forth good success. In Jesus' name. Amen.

74

Prayer for Friends

SHELLEY M. FISHER, PH.D.

Dear Heavenly Father, we praise and worship you, and thank you for friendship. You are a friend who sticks closer than a brother. Your Word says an unreliable friend brings ruin. Father, we need your discernment in choosing our friends, and we thank you that you no longer call us servants, but you call us friends.

Father, we give you our relationships and ask you to bring us the friends needed to get to our destiny. May the agape love of the Lord Jesus Christ shine through our friendships. Your Word tells us that good friends must be wisely chosen (Prov. 12:26). Father, we nurture friendships with people who have similar goals of wanting to please you by serving and building the kingdom.

We affirm Luke 6:31: "Do to others as you would have them do to you." We do nothing out of selfish ambition or vain conceit, rather in humility; we value others above ourselves. Father, we trust in you and do good. Thank you for your Word that says, "Two people are better off than one, for they can help each other succeed" (Eccl. 4:9–12). In Jesus' name. Amen.

75

Prayer for the Supernatural

❦

SHELLEY M. FISHER, PH.D.

The word in Jeremiah 33:3 says "Call unto Me, . . . and I will show you great and mighty things, that you know not of." Father God, your Word tells us that you are a Spirit and we are to worship you in spirit and in truth. You are Lord of Lords and King of Kings.

Father, we acknowledge your deity and your supernatural power. We thank you for moving in our affairs, not by power nor by might, but by your spirit. Amos 3:7 says, "Surely the Lord God will do nothing, but he reveals his secret to his servants, he prophets." We thank you that the Holy Spirit, the Paraclete, the third person of the Godhead is our helper, and comes alongside us to help and to develop us spiritually.

We thank you for loving us so much that you allow your words that we speak to commission our angels. For it is written: "Are they not ministering angels, send forth to minister for them who are heirs of salvation?" (Heb. 1:14).

Father, we worship you in spirit and in truth through praise and worship, your Word, using the name of Jesus, and applying the blood of Jesus. In Jesus' name. Amen.

76

Prayer for Dreams, Visions, and Visitations

❧

SHELLEY M. FISHER, PH.D.

I will pour out of My spirit upon all flesh; and your sons and your daughters shall prophesy, and your young men shall see visions, and your old men shall dream dreams. (Acts 2:17)

Father, in the name of Jesus, we praise and worship you. We give you the praise, the glory, and honor. Thank you for your relationship. Thank you that with our measure of faith, we see beyond our natural eyes into the spirit realm where you are working all things out for our good. Lord God, thank you for meeting us where we are, for every miracle, sign, and wonder, even every whisper when you said: "This is the way, walk therein" (Isa. 30:21). We thank you for your undying love, for your consistency, and for your faithfulness. What a mighty God you are!

We thank you for being a God of increase, of higher heights and deeper depths in you for the building of the kingdom. Father God, you wish that no man should perish, but that all men shall be saved. Give us wisdom to minister to your people, to go into the highways and byways and compel them to come and be saved. Thank you for instructing us in the mysteries of the kingdom so that men, women, boys, and girls will come running asking what must I do to be saved?

Lord, may we stay in a relationship to hear your voice and understand your ways. We desire to be kingdom builders. Destiny awaits to be fulfilled according to your Word: "I know the plans I think toward you says the Lord, plans of good, and not of evil to give you a future and a hope, an expected end." Thank you, Lord, for allowing us to be co-laborers with you.

Lord, give us dreams, visions, and visitations to enter into the spirit realm to serve mankind. In Jesus' name. Amen.

77

Prayer to End Disasters/ Calamities

∾

SHELLEY M. FISHER, PH.D.

F ather God, we give you glory, praise, and honor. We worship you for you are Lord of Lords and King of Kings. The
Word tells us to come boldly to the throne of grace to find grace
and mercy to help in time of need. We come to the throne in a
stance of victory for Jesus paid the price for our sins on Calvary.
We repent of sins in accordance with your promise in First John:
"If we come confessing our sins, you are faithful to forgive us and
to cleanse us from all unrighteousness" (1 John 1:9). By faith we
receive your forgiveness.

Father, we came in urgency against the prince of the power
of the air.

Satan, we bind you and your cohorts. We uproot Covid-19,
coronavirus, calamity, and other disasters. We dethrone you and
lift high the name of Jesus.

Devil, we attack you from our position of authority seated with
Jesus in the highest heavens at the right hand of God the Father.

The Word says the curse does not alight without a cause, but
as believers we have been redeemed from the curse of the Law
according to Galatians 3:13. Devil, we serve you notice that every
legal right we have given you over our families, land, nation, world,
and its people consciously and unconsciously is broken now in
the name of Jesus. We destroy and uproot you with the blood of

Jesus Christ and the finished work of the Cross. We release the Holy Spirit to destroy every blueprint of destruction in the name of Jesus.

God is able to do exceedingly abundantly above all that we can ask or think. We speak of destruction to the enemy's camp, and believe our request is answered in Jesus' name.

78

Prayer for Family and Friendships

⟨✳⟩

ERNESTINE MEADOWS MAY

Father, we thank you that you are the ultimate and Most High in Lordship, our heavenly Father. We are so thankful that you are so mindful of us. Your Word proves you as you say to us, to cast all our cares upon you, for you care for us, and your love is everlasting and without conditions. We recognize your grace and your mercy as being your offering of your promises given to us to perform and make your Word manifest that by faith it shall be done. We thank you that your Word as you send it out, it shall not return to you void, but will accomplish all that you proposed it to do. We trust and believe all things contained therein.

We thank you that family has been ordained by you and your Word reveals that family is important to you. Father, you command the honor of father and mother by children to obey them and listen to their instruction, your love provides everlasting goodness to generations as your commandments are remembered and kept by those who love you. We pray that fathers will bring up their children with discipline and to teach them your way, Lord. We confirm your Word, in our hearts, that, "But as for me and my house, we will serve the Lord"(Josh. 20:14).

We thank you that Jesus is our ultimate friend, as we pray that you will help us show the love He has for each of us through His commandment to love one another as He has loved us. What

263

manner of man would lay down his life for a friend? We bless the name of the Lord.

Thank you, Father, that you have accepted us into the beloved. We believe that you hear and answer every prayer of the heart and the spoken and written ones contained in these readings, In the name of Jesus, the Christ. Amen.

79

Prayer for the Supernatural

∽✢∾

ERNESTINE MEADOWS MAY

Father God, we thank you for your Word. We declare this Word to take root in our hearts and souls to accomplish what you have purposed for us and as we've read in your Word we further declare, "We will be strong in the Lord and in the power of His might" (Eph. 6:10).

We thank you that we put on the armor of salvation, and we commit to stand against the wiles of the enemy and by no means shall anything come against us. For the weapons of our warfare are not carnal, but mighty through God and equal to the pulling down of strongholds. We thank you for your supernatural hand of protection, and by faith, we receive, believe, and trust the promise of your Word.

We thank you for dreams, visions, and visitations from the Holy Spirit. We welcome your precious glory! We know that in all things and with all things, you are ever present. In every corner of darkness, you are with us; in every trial and tribulation, you have made a way of escape from the enemy and have provided an expected end for our victory. For yea, in all things we are overcomers because you have already caused us to overcome by the precious blood of Jesus and by the witness of our testimonies.

We declare and decree that we will hide under the shadow of the Almighty and we thank you that you give your angels to watch over, protect, and keep us always.

We thank you, Father. In the name of Jesus. Amen.

80

Prayer for Giving and Provision

$\curvearrowleft\!\!\times\!\!\curvearrowright$

ERNESTINE MEADOWS MAY

F ather, we thank you for your many blessings toward us all. We thank you for the authority and power of your Word in all things pertaining to life and all godliness. Thank you, Father, for our many readers; and we ask you to supply their every need according to your riches and glory by Christ Jesus. We thank you for giving them the desires of their hearts.

In all things, we give you honor, glory, and power as we invite you to be present in our every plan, purpose, and the choices we make regarding our daily lives. How awesome that you know our every need and we cast all of our cares upon you, for you care so much for us and love us so faithfully and unconditionally.

We thank you for your Word as we boldly proclaim its work for us. For greater is He that is in us than He that is in the world. We declare that you are omnipresent, being in all places and seeing all things. We thank you that there is nothing lost or hidden from you and that you will direct us by your spirit to recover all that has been lost, taken, stolen, or falsely manipulated from us. You are the God of restoration and supply, and we give you thanks for your provisions, even during this season of pandemic uncertainty. We trust you through it all as you bring us into the newness you are creating in our hearts, souls, and spirit for this set time and always.

In the name of Jesus we pray. Amen.

81

Prayer to Be Overcomers by the Word

❦

ERNESTINE MEADOWS MAY

Father, we thank you for another opportunity to come boldly into your gates with thanksgiving in our hearts and into your courts with praise. You are worthy, O Lord, to receive glory, honor, majesty, and power, for you alone have created all things and for thy pleasure all things are and were created. We praise you and we glorify your name in all the earth!

Father, we thank you for the authority of your Word. Your Word in us works for our good and we hide your Word in our hearts that we might not sin against you. What joy and glory that you have given your Word and yet you stand fast on your promise to perform that which you have purposed for our lives and all things pertaining to life and godliness.

We thank you that by your Word we run through a troop and leap over walls, we call for a mountain to be moved by our faith to believe and thus, speak out of the power of the Word that whatsoever thing we speak it shall come to pass. We overcome the adversary by the precious blood of the Lamb and the witness of our testimony. It is so!

We are brave and courageous, for the Lord our God shall be with us wherever we may go. If we ascend, He is there with us; if we should descend into the pits, He is also there with us! Thank you, Father God, that you have made a way of escape in all our adverse circumstances and situations. Thank you that in all things we overcome and victorious through Jesus Christ. In Him we pray. Amen.

82

Prayers for the Classroom of Life

$\backsim \! \times \! \curvearrowright$

ERNESTINE MEADOWS MAY

Heavenly Father, we thank you and praise you for your wondrous works in all the earth. We thank you that you have ordained us to live in the time in which we now live and that you call us to the attention of your good will for the kingdom and for each other.

We thank you for your vision in the things you have called us to do. By faith we have accepted to hear the call to respond to this project, "Sisters of The Gift". You sowed the seed of thought long before it was written by author contributors. I thank you that early one morning in the year 2010, February 8th, the vision was given as an idea for this book, as recorded through a journal hidden away in my secret place, that has come into fruition. Now I pray that you will receive the glory from these readers and responders to your word.

We thank you that in all things we trust you for our portion, for our sustainability, our supply, and our needs. We thank you that all things are made well when we believe the promises given in your Word. We declare that your grace is sufficient, and your mercies are available to us every day.

We offer up to you every care and concern that needs your blessing whether it is physical, mental, or spiritual. We thank you also, that you give us the desires of our hearts.

We pray for those who desire healing, deliverance, finances, family members, employment, and just a refreshing of energy and strength.

We thank you for your Word in us and it will always work for us. We are determined to speak your Word boldly to affirm your will in us. We declare that thy will be done in us, in our families, our government, the body of Christ, in the needs we have now concerning world needs, those in authority, and for the peace of Jerusalem, as you have given us to pray.

In the name of Jesus. Amen

83

Prayer to Acknowledge God's Faithfulness

∽✦∾

GLORIA SHARPE SMITH

Lord God, I thank you for the power of your Word. Thank you for being faithful to your Word. You watch over it to bring it to pass, just as you would have it; and for this, I'm grateful. I ask now that you continue to strengthen us with the desire to know your Word, to study your Word, to speak your Word and to do all in confidence. Thank You now for a new boldness in our spirits. We pray that your Spirit, the Spirit of the living God, will rise up within us. We pray for opportunities to speak your Word without fear and to stand in the truth of knowing that you are God, and that you have all power and authority in your hands. There is no need to fear or to fret over anything. We bind the spirit of worry and frustration; we speak truth and life with confidence and boldness in the name of Jesus. Thank You, Lord, that you elevate us from faith to faith. We are growing from glory to glory. Thank You for people around the world who are being delivered and set free from the bondage of fear because your Word says: "Whom the Son sets free, is free indeed." Thank You, Lord God for the freedom we have to worship, to praise, to serve, to love, and to be who you have called and equipped us to be. Thank You now for the joy that serving you brings; and thank you, God, that we can face each new day with a heart of gratitude and a positive attitude. This is our prayer in Jesus' name. Amen!

84

Prayer for Reflecting

GLORIA SHARPE SMITH

Our Father, and my God, thank you for this day. Thank you for being a loving, caring, compassionate Father. Thank you for being concerned about everything that concerns your children. You are a good Father and I want to say thank you and I appreciate you. I appreciate you for all that you've done, what you're doing, and what your Word promises that you're going to do. Father, thank you for the love that you have provided for me and for your people. It gives us the assurance that you love us. You've given us your peace, your grace, your mercy, and you shower favor and goodness upon us. My heart is overwhelmed with gratitude. When I consider all that you've done, my joy is complete. It's your Word, Lord God, that helps us to get a glimpse of the love that you have for everyone. So, I'm asking you to give us a deeper understanding and love for your Word. Your Word is precious. Help us to hide it in my heart, so that we may not sin against you. Right now, I'm asking for your help in strengthening me in your Word and in the love for your Word. I thank you that you help us to live a life of faith, based on the power that's in the name of Jesus. I ask that you help us to rightly divide your Word and to know it as truth and to live it out as you would have us live. Help us to have confidence, strength and boldness as we live out the plans that you have for us. Thank you for grace and the assurance that the plan you have for us is perfect. No matter where life may take us, you will be with us.

Father, I trust you with all of my being and acknowledge that you are faithful, even when I don't understand the plan. Even when the path seems unclear, and the tests seem difficult, please grant us the peace that only you can provide. Our heart's desire is to hear you say, well done!

In Jesus' name. Amen.

85

Prayer for Blessings Bestowed

❧

GLORIA SHARPE SMITH

Lord God, thank you for the many blessings that you have bestowed upon us. I acknowledge that all good and perfect gifts come from you. Thank you for teaching us how to give and have a spirit of giving. You have taught me how to receive and to do good. I just want to give thanks to you for the power and the presence of the Holy Spirit who leads, guides, and directs. I thank you for the voice of the Holy Spirit that whispers in my ear that all is well. Thank you for the joy that comes with giving. It is through your love, and giving us your son, Jesus, that we are able to give. I ask and thank you for opportunities to be a blessing to others.

Help us to have compassion and to be quick to recognize a need and to meet it according to your provisions. Help us to see victory in every situation and fully understand that the battles that we encounter in life are yours, and they are for our good!

Thank you for your plan of salvation that offers and promises us a life of love, grace, peace, freedom, favor, hope, and joy in you! Grant us the measure of faith to believe it. In Jesus' name. Amen

86

Prayer for Facing Fear

Gloria Sharpe Smith

Lord, your Word says that you have not given us a spirit of fear, but of power and of love and of a sound mind. Thank you for those words and for the comfort and encouragement that they provide. We ask that you let them be ingrained in our spirits and bring them to our remembrance when we're faced with the unfamiliar. Help us to live a life that honors you: one of courage and confidence in you. Grant us the boldness to live out our faith and fully embrace the glory of living and experiencing life in the supernatural realm of your love and power. When we feel weak, reassure us that it is in your strength that we are strong. When we feel lonely, remind us that we are yours and that you're with us with every breath that we take. When we have doubts, remind us that you specialize in the impossible and there's nothing that you can't do. When we feel weary and tired, remind us that you are a rewarder of those who diligently seek you. When we're tempted to think of lack, remind us that it's your desire for us to prosper and be in health as our souls prosper. Help us to acknowledge each day as a gift and remind us that tomorrow never comes, but that our future is bright. Father, hold on to us. Help us to live in the "now," knowing that we can count our blessings and recognize that you are good. Your grace is sufficient, and your love will never fail!

This is our prayer. In Jesus' name. Amen

87

Prayer for Gratitude

❧

Gloria Sharpe Smith

It is possible to give away and become richer! It is also possible to hold on too tightly and lose everything. Yes, the liberal man shall be rich! By watering others, he waters himself. (Prov. 11:24 TLV)

Lord, teach us to be givers. Let us not become so attached to anything in this world that we would hold back from reflecting on your generosity towards us. Help us to give freely of our time, talents, resources, and words of encouragement. Whatever it is that you have blessed us with, help us to view it loosely, so that we can release it for the good of another without counting the cost.

Help us to trust that whatever we give away, it's possible with you to restore even more.

Help us to always be reminded that you encourage us to cast our bread upon the waters, knowing that it will be returned to us. Help us to have the confidence in knowing that you will meet all of our needs according to your riches in glory by Christ Jesus and that you will not withhold any good thing from us. Help us and show us ways to sow kindness and generosity to others, so that we may be a blessing.

We are grateful for a spirit of generosity, and we thank you for meeting all of our needs according to your overwhelming abundance of blessings. Lord, we pray that whatever gifts we offer will be acceptable in your sight. We pray you will honor them and that you will be pleased, as we give back to you. We trust your faithfulness in honoring your Word.

In Jesus' name. Amen

Author Biographies

Gloria Sharpe Smith

Gloria Sharpe Smith is a retired educator and consultant for a major publishing company. She also worked as a facilitator for the Indiana Department of education. She earned a Bachelor of Science and a Master of Science degree from Indiana University Northwest in Gary, Indiana. In addition, she holds a Certificate of Ministry from the United Christian Church and Ministries Association. She has a love and passion for the Word of God and the power of prayer. Gloria is the founder of Truthful Conversations,Inc. a Bible-based, Non Profit Organization that concentrates on helping others experience victory in life through the truth of God's Word. Because of her Christian walk, she has become an esteemed spiritual advisor and mentor to many young people throughout the nation. She is often a guest speaker for various Christian fellowships, conferences, programs, and retreats. She has a heart for missions and marvels at the way God chooses to use her in His plan for reaching people and demonstrating His love through service with compassion. She has traveled extensively throughout North America, Europe, Asia, and Africa. She has visited both Egypt and Senegal twice on missionary trips. Gloria is dedicated to serving people with the love of Christ. She lives in Sugar Land, Texas, and enjoys lavishing love and giving attention to her two miniature pinchers, Melody and Reign. She's grateful for fifty-two years of marriage to Ernest T. Smith before his passing. They have two sons and three grandchildren. Her next project will be a work celebrating the highlights and lessons learned from fifty-two years of marriage.

Gloria would love for you to reach out with comments and questions!

Email: truthfulconvo@gmail.com

www.gloriasharpesmith.com

Special Acknowledgements:

To my typist, Sonya Henderson: Thank you so much for your patience, perseverance, and availability. You typed, you read, and you supplied great feedback. NuNu loves and appreciates you so much!

To my reader, Lexxus Armani Macias: Thank you for reading my stories, making valuable comments, and encouraging your grandmother to become a writer. Granddaughters are a very special gift from God! I'm glad He gave me you.

To my editor, Melanie Stiles : I thank God for the blessing that you have been on this project. You said that I could use fewer words to tell my stories, and that my readers would connect with what was coming from my heart. I'm trusting your expertise.

To my technical assistant, Kelly May: Thank you for being an answer to prayer right in the nick of time!

Of Special Note—I would like to thank the following wonderful people for their support and enthusiastic cooperation in volunteering to share their stories: **Beverly Bryant, Samuel Ighalo, Sandra Ighalo, Dot Pitt, Anthony D. (Tony) Smith, Michael Taylor, and Sheree Zampino.**

Shelley M. Fisher, Ph.D.

D r. Shelley M. Fisher's passion is to see people reach their destiny. She believes all people have greatness within just waiting to be unleashed. While meandering through the twists and turns of life there are challenges and obstacles that can hinder growth. She believe that information, inspiration, nurturing, and mentoring can help people realize their greatness. The path to overcoming is not just for a chosen few, but for everyone. Her childhood ambition of teaching is still being fulfilled as Dr. Fisher teaches, preaches, leads, and facilitates groups. As an elementary teacher, when a struggling student finally "got it" (understood), she was elated. Being intuitive has helped her in relating to others and in problem-solving situations. Her life's tapestry has been woven by a myriad of experiences as a principal and a professor, a chaplain and a consultant, a woman and a wife, a minister and a mother, and both a lifetime teacher and a lifetime student. She has always had a love for reading and writing.

A lifetime of journaling has assuaged her fears and doubts, as well as, allowed her to celebrate successes and victories. An entrepreneurial spirit has led her into a variety of pursuits: www. shelleymfisherbooks.com and a real estate investor, *Fisher Solutions, LLC.* Matriculations include: Indiana University, Bloomington, Indiana, (Bachelor and Master of Science in Education); Purdue University Northwest, (Certification in Administration); Loyola

University of Chicago, (Mentor Certification, One who can lead you through life experiences using the Bible as the focal point); Regent University, Virginia Beach, Virginia, (Doctor of Philosophy, Ph.D.) in Organizational Leadership.

Publications:
Nehemiah on Leadership, I Can't Come Down; Junia Arise (co-author); *Go and Tell— Spiritual Checkup: Does What You Do and Say Align? Praying Prolific Prayers with Signatures of Prolific Women* (co-author) A children's genre: *Dad, Me, and the Pandemic.*

She resides in Gary, Indiana, and is married to Alfred Fisher. They have two children, Tiffiny and Eric, and two grandchildren, Kamari and Erica.

Ernestine M. May

Ernestine May is a retired school educator and administrator. She grew up in a small rural town located at Biscoe, Arkansas. She has authored a chronology of her life from "meager to eager" in her memoir, *Life Is a Story* (2009).

She earned an A.A. Degree (Associated Arts) from Shorter Jr. College in North Little Rock, and a B. S. Degree from Arkansas, Mechanical and Normal College, now known as University of Arkansas at Pine Bluff, with a minor in English. Moving to Gary, Indiana, she matriculated at Indiana University NW to receive her M.S. Degree in Elementary Education, with a double minor: one in English and another in African American Studies. She received licensure in Teaching and Administration from the State of Indiana and from Nevada. She was licensed as a traditional teacher as well as a guest teacher during her time as a facilitator for kindergarten children.

She has traveled to Ghana, West Africa, with a cadre of teachers led by Dr. Asante, an expert in the field of African American Studies, where teachers collaborated with other constituents in the field of education. Her journey also led her to Beijing, China, where she visited with educators from five countries there to study, *Play in Education for Children,* under the leadership of Dr. Mack Brown and under the auspices of People to People, implemented by the late President Dwight D. Eisenhower. Along the path of teaching early elementary aged children she pursued her interest in studying and became certified in Montessori Methods from Meca-Seton Training Center in Hinsdale, Illinois, under the Director and Founder, Celma P. Perry Ph.D., São Paulo, Brasil.

Children became an integral part of her life, having four of her own: Andre, Don, Kelly, and Mona with six grandchildren, and five great grands to brag about. She did not stop there; she hosted, along with husband, Floyd, a total of six foreign exchange students from four continents: Africa, Asia, Europe, and South America. Cultural and extended opportunities for Ernestine May have created her to become a catalyst for dialogue to offer positive experiences for others as she too is here to put a sword in the earth to let the world know that she was here and is leaving a legacy of hope as her contribution for a better tomorrow.

It gives her great pleasure to honor her Father, to know Him and make Him known to others by her inspirational writings, giving others that same hope for a better tomorrow as she leaves this legacy to herald the Faith that brought her from the fields of a share-cropping plantation to where she is today!

Doretha G. Rouse

Doretha Rouse grew up in Memphis, Tennessee, and moved to Gary, Indiana, to work as an elementary school teacher. She presently resides in Gary, Indiana. Beyond her classroom she served as teacher leader coordinating math and science fairs. She led in decorations and created props for school plays, as well as served as the local teachers' union representative.

Doretha Rouse was an avid tennis player. Her athleticism was shown in her winning tennis competitions in her then home state of Tennessee. She is gregarious and enjoys meeting and helping people. The call to community leadership was answered when she was elected to the citywide School Board. She likes singing and has directed the choir, "JOY." Ms. Rouse sings in an ecumenical citywide choir. Speaking at women's conferences and churches is one of her favorite pastimes. Her passion is prayer and she is an "acclaimed" Prayer Warrior and desires to see people victorious in life. Her signature Scripture is 2 Chronicles 7:14: "If my people who are called by my name will humble themselves and pray..." Doretha has a Master of Science degree in Education from Indiana University and a Bachelor of Science in Education from Tennessee State University. She was married to Frahn Rouse for many years, and they are the parents of two children and three grandchildren. Doretha is recently widowed and is grateful for her walk with God through the years.

CPSIA information can be obtained
at www.ICGtesting.com
Printed in the USA
LVHW050122200422
716645LV00014B/476

9 781662 841569